ARIZONA

ARIZONA BY ROAD

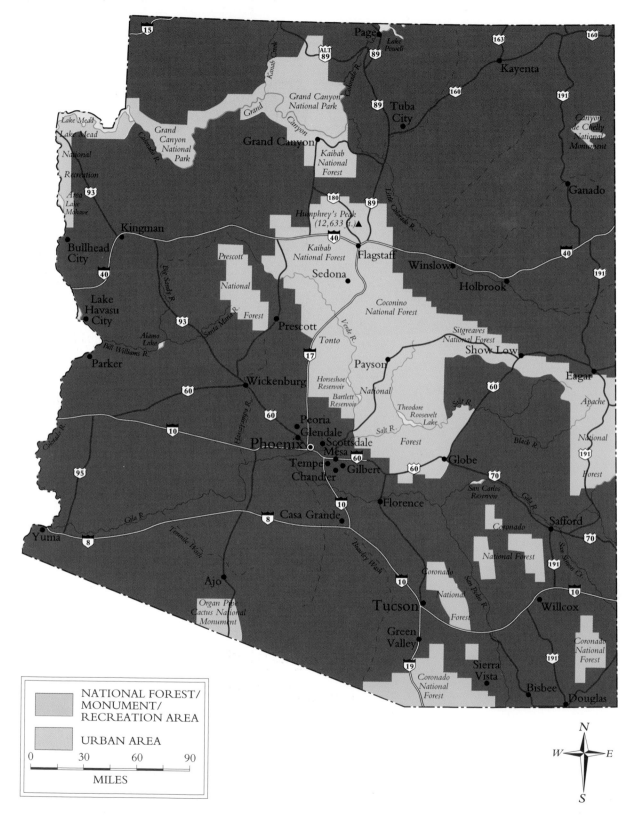

NATIONAL FOREST/
MONUMENT/
RECREATION AREA

URBAN AREA

0   30   60   90

MILES

CELEBRATE THE STATES
ARIZONA

Melissa McDaniel

BENCHMARK BOOKS

MARSHALL CAVENDISH
NEW YORK

Benchmark Books
Marshall Cavendish Corporation
99 White Plains Road
Tarrytown, New York 10591-9001

Library of Congress Cataloging-in-Publication Data

McDaniel, Melissa.
Arizona / Melissa McDaniel.
p.   cm. — (Celebrate the states)
Includes bibliographical references and index.
Summary: Discusses the geographic features, history, government,
people, and attractions of the state of Arizona
ISBN 0-7614-0647-6
1. Arizona—Juvenile literature. [1. Arizona.] I. Title. II. Series.
F811.3 .M38   2000   979.1—dc21   00-022486

Maps and graphics supplied by Oxford Cartographers, Oxford, England

Photo Research by Candlepants Incorporated

Cover Photo: The Image Bank / D. Carroll

The photographs in this book are used by permission and through the courtesy of; *The Image Bank* : Alvis
Upitis, 6-7; Simon Wilkinson, 16; A.T. Willet, 18, 30; Dann Coffey, 22; Pete Turner, 27; Phillip Kretchmar, 60;
G. Kenny; Harald Sund, 64; Bullaty Lomeo, 72; Ira Block, 75; T. Stableford, 82; Joe Devenney, 108;
Place, 112; Andrea Pistolesi, 135; Gill C. Kenny, back cover. *Photo Researchers Inc.*: Jim Corwin, 10-11, 52-53;
G.C. Kelly, 19; Rod Planck, 20; Kjell Sandved, 77; Harold Hoffman, 105;George Ranalli, 111; CK Lorenz,
117(right and left), 120. *Corbis* : Marc Muench, 15; Tom Brakefield, 23; David Muench, 24, 29, 102, 103;
Jay Dickman, 106; Ted Streshinsky, 57; Jim Sugar, 65; Tony Roberts, 67; Patrick Bennett, 68-69; Michael S.
Yamashita, 73; Kevin Fleming, 84-85; Rueters, 88; Dave G. Houser, 93, 99; Tom Bean, 96-97; Galen Rowell,
115; Pacha, 126; Bettmann/UPI,127, 128,132(top).*Norma Jean Gargasz* : 58, 76, 79, 81, 123, 124.
The Thomas Gilcrease Institute of American History and Art, Tulsa Oklahoma: 32-33. *Arizona Historical
Society,Tucson*: 35,37, 38, 41, 42. *Archive Photos*: 40, 50, 87, 131,132 (lower); Gordon M. Grant,92;
Bob Parent, 129; Rueters/Gary Hershorne,130. *National Archives*: 44. *Bisbee Mining and Historical Museum*: 46.
University of Arizona, Special Collections: 49. *Lowell Observatory*: 91.

Printed in Italy

1   3   5   6   4   2

CONTENTS

ARIZONA IS . . .

Arizona is hot . . .

The temperature "remains at a constant 120 degrees in the shade, except when it varies and goes higher."   —humorist Mark Twain

. . . and it is prickly.

"It has been said, and truly, that everything in the desert either stings, stabs, stinks, or sticks. You will find the flora here as venomous, hooked, barbed, thorny, prickly, needled, saw-toothed, hairy, stickered, mean, bitter, sharp, wiry, and fierce as animals."

—naturalist Edward Abbey

Arizona overwhelms the senses . . .

It is "all very beautiful and magical here—a quality which cannot be described. You have to live it and breathe it, let the sun bake into you."   —photographer Ansel Adams

. . . with its strange beauty.

"Vegetation is not needed to produce beauty in the land for the earth herself is many-hued, streaked with strange bright sands and clays and walled with mountains of rich-hued rock."

—poet and historian Sharlot Hall

Arizona is a young state . . .

"The promising Metropolis of Arizona consisted of three chimneys and a coyote."   —journalist J. Ross Browne, 1864

"If you've been in Phoenix a year, you're an old-timer."

—journalist John Gunther, 1947

. . . that once attracted dreamers . . .

"From the East came people from all walks of life. They traveled by stagecoach, wagon, railroad, horseback, and some even came afoot. They came, all of them, in search of a dream in one form or another. . . . It was really the West that brought them, the love of adventure, the wild, free life."   —historian Marshall Trimble

. . . who wanted to start life anew.

Arizona was "a blank slate on which they could etch their visions of the future."   —historian Thomas E. Sheridan

Today, people come for the good life.

"The quality of life brings people here. A friend of mine got in his car once and drove up to Roosevelt Lake to water-ski, then headed up to Flagstaff to snow ski. All in one day."   —Senator John McCain

---

Arizona is jagged mountains, gaping canyons, and severe deserts. Its uncompromising landscape made it one of the last states to be settled by white Americans. From the time fortune seekers first scrambled through its hills in search of gold and silver, it has been a place to reinvent oneself and get a fresh start on life. Arizona holds out that promise still.

1 DESERT AND CANYON

Mention Arizona and most people think of two things: the Grand Canyon and the desert. But Arizona is much more than this. The state boasts several deserts and thousands of canyons. In between are mountains and buttes, waterfalls and pine forests, creating a dazzling and diverse landscape unrivaled by any other state.

CANYON COUNTRY

Still, the most famous landform in Arizona, indeed, in the entire country, is the Grand Canyon. This vast chasm cuts across northwestern Arizona. Its eroded pillars, sheer cliffs, and crumbly slopes are dressed in muted colors. Watching the play of light and shadow and how the oranges and greens and rusts subtly change as the sun crosses the sky are the real pleasures of the canyon. The Grand Canyon is so huge it is hard to comprehend. "Pick any little section of it," says one visitor, "and think about it. It's actually a cliff a thousand feet high. And below it is another, and another, and another. It boggles the mind."

Size alone can't explain the canyon's allure. Other canyons are deeper and more rugged, but none can equal the Grand Canyon in sheer majesty. After naturalist John Muir visited the canyon in 1898, he said, "No matter how far you have wandered hitherto, or how many famous gorges and valleys you have seen, this one, the

LAND AND WATER

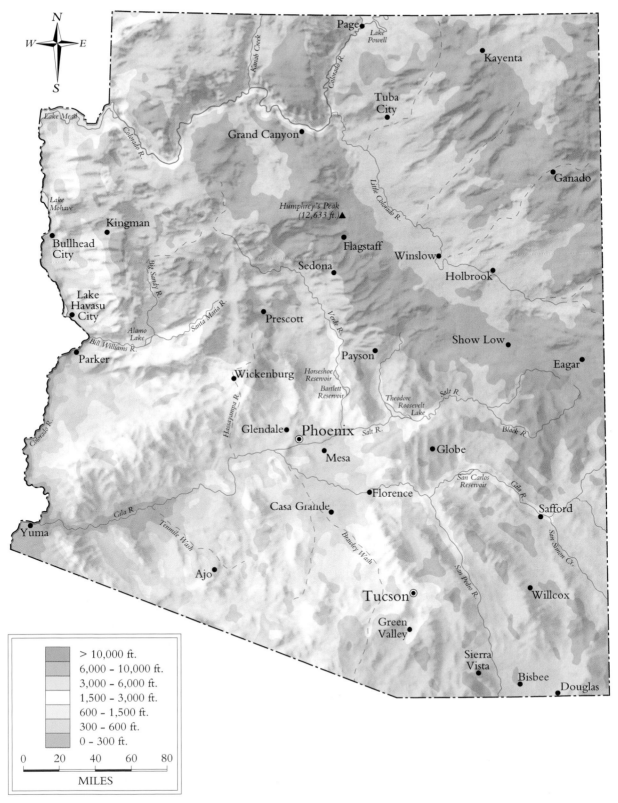

N
W · E
S

Page
Lake Powell
Kayenta
Tuba City
Lake Mead
Colorado R.
Grand Canyon
Ganado
Lake Mohave
Humphrey's Peak (12,633 ft.) ▲
Kingman
Flagstaff
Winslow
Bullhead City
Sedona
Holbrook
Colorado R.
Little Colorado R.
Kanab Creek
Big Sandy R.
Lake Havasu City
Santa Maria R.
Alamo Lake
Prescott
Verde R.
Show Low
Eagar
Bill Williams R.
Parker
Payson
Wickenburg
Horseshoe Reservoir
Bartlett Reservoir
Salt R.
Theodore Roosevelt Lake
Black R.
Hassayampa R.
Glendale
Phoenix
Salt R.
Globe
Mesa
San Carlos Reservoir
Gila R.
Florence
Safford
Colorado R.
Casa Grande
San Simon Cr.
Gila R.
Tenmile Wash
Yuma
Bradley Wash
San Pedro R.
Ajo
Tucson
Willcox
Green Valley
Sierra Vista
Bisbee
Douglas

> 10,000 ft.
6,000 – 10,000 ft.
3,000 – 6,000 ft.
1,500 – 3,000 ft.
600 – 1,500 ft.
300 – 600 ft.
0 – 300 ft.

0   20   40   60   80
MILES

Grand Canyon of the Colorado, will seem as novel to you, as unearthly in the color and grandeur and quantity of its architecture, as if you had found it after death, on some other star."

More than five thousand feet below the canyon's rim, what looks like a tiny stream is actually the mighty Colorado River. It was the coursing Colorado that carved the 277 miles of the Grand Canyon to the depths it is today. But it was rain and snowmelt and streams that gave the canyon its width—as much as eighteen miles—and carved its spectacular shapes.

The land here is soft and dry, so water erodes it quickly and dramatically. The same is true all across northern Arizona, where water has chiseled thousands of canyons of every shape and size. Some are lush mountain gorges. Others are slot canyons, just a few feet wide, but with sandstone cliffs that tower a thousand feet above the dusty ground.

MOUNTAINS AND FORESTS

South of the Grand Canyon are the San Fransisco Peaks, which include Humphreys Peak, the state's highest point at 12,633 feet. These rugged mountains are a far cry from the typical image of Arizona. Here, thick forests of Douglas fir and white fir provide dark, damp homes for black bears and mountain lions. The region also boasts the world's largest stand of soaring ponderosa pine. Much of central Arizona is mountainous. The cool peaks of the White, Mazatzal, and other ranges entice hikers and fishers and anyone else who wants a bit of relief from the heat. Slashing across this region is a peculiar formation called the Mogollon Rim. Here,

A skier takes advantage of a beautiful day in the San Francisco Mountains.

the land suddenly drops two thousand feet. This steep, heavily forested cliff serves as a boundary between northern Arizona and the desert regions to the south.

FOUR DESERTS

For all its magnificent forests and chasms, the fact remains that more than half of Arizona is desert. But again, Arizona surprises, because it has not one desert, but four.

The Mohave Desert, in the northwest, is the state's bleakest desert and its dryest, receiving only four to five inches of rain a year. Barren brown hills stretch off into the distance. Sometimes, the only plant life visible is creosote, a scrubby evergreen bush that seems able to withstand anything. Creosotes are remarkably hardy: scientists think some of them are 11,000 years old. This means that somewhere out there is a creosote bush that is the oldest living thing on Earth.

In northeastern Arizona is the Great Basin Desert, a fascinating region of eroded canyons, hills, and buttes. Its most famous stretch is Monument Valley, where strange, isolated rock formations rise

Late in the day, the spires at Monument Valley are a burning red.

from the surrounding flatlands. Once, the entire area was as tall as the "monuments" are today, but over time, the sandstone splintered, crumbled, and washed away. All that is left today are the jagged red spires.

In Arizona's southeastern corner is the Chihuahuan Desert. This is the high desert, where the sharp spears of the yucca plant rise from the grasses that take root there.

The jewel of the Arizona deserts is the Sonoran, which spreads across most of the southern third of the state. This is the desert that comes to mind when you think of Arizona, the one of towering saguaro cacti, their arms reaching toward the sky. The Sonoran Desert hosts a larger variety of plants and animals than any other desert in North America. Indeed, it is the only one with areas so thick with trees they can actually be called forests. The Sonoran is filled with mesquite, paloverde, brittlebush, ocotillo, and of course cactus galore—prickly pear, barrel, hedgehog, organ pipe.

The teddybear cholla gets its name because it is so covered with spines that it looks fuzzy. Far from cuddly, it is among the most ferocious cacti. Its spines are like fishhooks, with tiny barbs that jut backward. These barbs hold the spine in place when it sticks into your skin. Sometimes the only way to remove it is to pull it out with pliers. Always walk carefully in the desert.

Arizona's animals can be as dangerous as its plants. The state is home to eleven types of rattlesnake, thirty species of scorpions, and even the Gila monster, one of only two venomous lizards on Earth. Although the Gila monster has gained a reputation as a killer, its bite is not actually deadly, and it will only bite if it's being harassed.

Journalist Lawrence W. Cheek once wrote that deserts "teem with life—weird, colorful, perfectly adapted, interdependent, fiercely obstinate life." A good example is the Gila monster, one of only two poisonous lizards on the planet.

Of course, not all desert animals are poisonous. You'll also find jackrabbits, desert tortoises, bighorn sheep, and mice.

SKY ISLANDS

Even though you are surrounded by desert, no matter where you go in southern Arizona you can still see mountains. These mountains are sometimes called sky islands, because many animals living

A bicyclist soars through the air in the Sonoran Desert.

DESERT GIANTS

Nothing says Arizona like the saguaro. This towering cactus has become the symbol of the state, appearing on license plates and in advertisements. In movies, saguaros even show up among the dramatic buttes of Monument Valley, although they don't actually grow there. To filmmakers, Arizona equals saguaros, so they construct fake ones.

Saguaros grow only in the Sonoran Desert, where they provide homes for many other desert creatures. Gila woodpeckers and gilded flickers make holes in the cactus and nest there. Once they have raised their young, these birds move on. Then a cactus wren or an elf owl might move in. These holes make ideal homes, because it is often twenty degrees cooler inside a saguaro than outside in the blazing sun.

Saguaros are the giants of the desert, sometimes topping fifty feet. But it takes 150 years for them to grow that tall. Saguaros don't even sprout their first arms until they are about seventy-five.

It is the saguaros' arms that make them seem human. Especially when the light is low, saguaros can look like forlorn figures in the distance. Perhaps this is why Arizonans have taken them to heart. People still talk about the time a few years back when a man fired a shotgun at a saguaro. The cactus toppled onto the gunman, killing him. Many Arizonans felt sorrier for the saguaro.

on them are stuck there every bit as much as they would be if they were living on an island. For instance, the Chiricahua fox squirrel, which lives in the cool forests of the Chiricahua Mountains in southeastern Arizona, could never survive a trip across the hot, dry desert to another mountain. If development, pollution, or a forest fire destroyed their habitat, they could not simply move on. They'd never make it.

A trip up one of these mountains is like traveling from Mexico to Canada. Except instead of having to drive more than a thousand miles, you just have to drive a couple of miles up a snaking road. As you climb these mountains, some nearly 10,000 feet high, the landscape changes from rugged desert to cool forest. Indeed, the sky islands are some of the most diverse places in the United States. They are home to an amazing range of creatures, from tarantulas to bobcats to coatimundis, including sixty animal species found nowhere else. More than 250 species of birds find food and shelter in the sky islands. Many Mexican birds, such as the trogan and the painted redstart, never travel any farther into the United States.

HEAVEN AND HELL

There's no denying it—Arizona is hot. It's not a coincidence that Arizona boasts more places with hell in their name than any other state. There are fifty-five of them, ranging from Hell Hole Valley to Hellgate Mountain, not to mention four different Hell Canyons.

On average, Phoenix suffers through ninety-one days a year when the temperature breaks 100 degrees. The first sometimes hits in mid-April. "What have I done," moaned one transplant from

Sometimes the best way to deal with the fierce Arizona heat is to get wet.

THE JAGUAR RETURNS

"I never thought I'd see a jaguar," says Jack Childs. "I thought it was just something you talked about around the campfire." But in 1996, Childs came across one of these mighty cats in the Baboquivari Mountains in southern Arizona.

Jaguars are the largest cat in the Western Hemisphere. They sometimes grow eight feet long. Although these striking creatures once roamed throughout the Southwest, it was thought they had been eliminated from the United States. But a few months before Childs's sighting, rancher Warner Glenn encountered a jaguar along the Arizona–New Mexico border. He photographed it, providing the first evidence in a decade of a jaguar in the United States.

The jaguar "is here because he likes what he's found—plenty of game and not very many people, and that's the way we'd like to keep it," says Glenn. But no one is quite sure how to do that. More and more houses are being built in the region, and extensive cattle grazing has destroyed some grasslands. In a rare show of cooperation, environmental organizations, government agencies, and ranchers who own land in the area are working together to preserve the jaguars' habitat. Since jaguars living in southern Arizona likely cross and recross the border with Mexico, Mexican officials will also have to join in the effort if these extraordinary animals are to be protected.

HELL IN ARIZONA

It was part of the frontier spirit never to take oneself too seriously. So when the Arizona Booster said, "Arizona needs only water and climate to make it a paradise," the skeptical listener responded, "Yes, that's all hell needs, too."

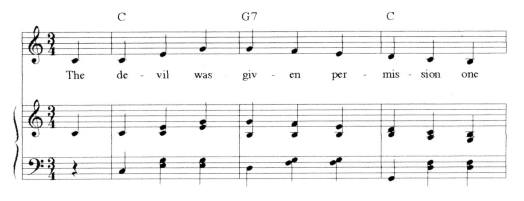

The de - vil was giv - en per - mis - sion one

day To se - lect him a land for his own spe - cial

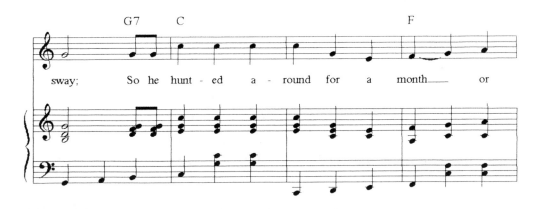

sway; So he hunt - ed a - round for a month____ or

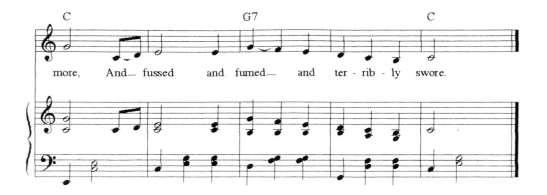

more, And— fussed and fumed— and ter - rib - ly swore.

He at last was delighted a country to view
Where the prickly pear and the mesquite grew.
With a survey brief, without further excuse,
He stood on the bank of the Santa Cruz.

He studded the land with the prickly pear,
And scattered the cactus everywhere;
The Spanish dagger, sharp-pointed and tall,
And at last the chollas to outstick them all.

He filled the river with sand 'til 'twas almost dry,
And poisoned the land with alkali;
And promised himself on its slimy brink
To control all who from it should drink.

He saw there was one improvement to make,
So he imported the scorpion, tarantula, and snake,
That all that might come to this country to dwell,
Would be sure to think it was almost hell.

He fixed the heat at a hundred and 'leven,
And banished forever the moisture from heaven;
And remarked as he heard his furnaces roar
That the heat might reach five hundred more.

Oregon the first time he saw the thermometer hit 116 degrees. In the days before air-conditioning, this sort of heat was insufferable. During summer, people would haul their beds outdoors. Wily Arizonans put the legs of the bed in buckets of water to keep scorpions from crawling into bed with them. Today, Arizonans cope by rarely venturing out into the oppressive heat. They move from air-conditioned house to air-conditioned car to air-conditioned office. Some only go outside for an early-morning round of golf or a refreshing dip in the pool at the day's end.

Many people believe June is the worst month in southern Arizona. It is not only hot but also bone dry. The ground hardens, plants shrivel, tempers flare. But then, in July and August, monsoon season hits. Some afternoons, thunderclouds roll in and dump buckets of rain on the parched land. Although the rains last only a few minutes, they bring blessed relief.

But these rains also bring danger, for the parched land cannot soak up that much water. Instead, the water courses down gullies and dry creek beds, sometimes creating dangerous flash floods. In 1997, twelve people were swept away by a flash flood while hiking in the bottom of Antelope Canyon, a slot canyon in northern Arizona. It was a beautiful day and not a drop of water had fallen in the canyon itself.

Winter sees milder rains and milder temperatures. In December and January in southern Arizona temperatures are in the sixties, with lows rarely dipping below freezing. For decades, Arizona's pleasant winters have been enticing visitors. Those who come get more than comfortable weather. Each evening, as the blinding light of day begins to fade, the sky puts on a dazzling show. It explodes

Arizona is famous for what novelist Barbara Kingsolver has called "five-alarm sunsets."

in pinks and peaches and purples, which change quickly, so that each minute prompts more oohs and aahs. Arizona sunsets are neon and technicolor. They act like magnets, drawing people out of their homes and luring motorists off the road to watch. No matter what you're doing, an Arizona sunset is always worth stopping for.

With the warm, dry spring come spectacular wildflower displays. Practically overnight, the muted browns and olive greens of the desert are overwhelmed by expanses of blue lupine or brilliant yellow desert marigold. "It's like a volcano of gold," exclaimed one man upon seeing the fields of Mexican gold poppies in Picacho Peak State Park.

After the wildflowers of March have faded, April and May bring dazzling cactus blossoms. The bright scarlet blooms that emerge from a tangle of spines on the claret cup cactus are almost as big as the plant itself. And at the end of the season, delicate white flowers bloom atop the giant saguaros, only to wilt after just one day.

Farther north in Arizona, the climate is much milder. Towns like Sedona and Prescott enjoy four distinct seasons, each of them pleasant. From the aspens blazing yellow against a brilliant blue autumn sky to the beautiful dustings of snow in the winter, Arizona can seem like heaven. A man who fled the frigid winters and humid summers of Chicago for Sedona explained his decision: "One word: weather."

DUST AND HAZE

It used to be that people moved to Arizona to enjoy the clean desert air. Few would do that today. "When I came here initially, I thought I would probably stay," says Jim Betz, who moved from California to Phoenix more than fifteen years ago. "Now, it's not even a consideration." All too often, a pillow of brown haze nestles against southern Arizona's jagged mountains. Much of this pollution comes from car and truck exhaust. And when tiny particles of dust

When wildflowers bloom in spring, an explosion of color overwhelms the normally brown land.

In the last hundred years, Phoenix has grown from a town of five thousand to the nation's sixth-largest city, with more than a million residents. Because of all these people and their cars, the region's once pristine air is often choked with smog.

and exhaust settle onto the road in Arizona's dry climate, they just get kicked back up into the air by cars driving over them.

More and more Arizonans are suffering from breathing problems, headaches, and stinging eyes, and many blame the pollution. "At least 100 days out of the year, it's bad enough to interfere with my work and recreation and just feeling decent," Betz says. Although Arizonans are using cleaner fuel, this won't solve the problem.

People would have to drive less for there to be fewer dust particles churned into the air, and that seems unlikely. Phoenix area residents drive 59 million miles a day, and that number is expected to rise by 50 percent in the next fifteen years. It remains to be seen whether Arizonans can find their way back to the clear blue skies that drew them there in the first place.

2 BECOMING ARIZONA

The Grand Canyon, by Thomas Moran

Arizona is a young state—it was the last of the lower forty-eight states to enter the Union. But humans have lived there for thousands of years, giving Arizona a rich and fascinating history.

THE FIRST ARIZONANS

The first people to arrive in what is now Arizona were hunters who wandered into the area 15,000 years ago. They stalked the camels, bison, antelope, and other large animals that thrived on what was then the region's grassy plains.

As the climate grew drier, deserts replaced grasslands. The large animals died off, and the people turned to gathering nuts and berries and hunting smaller animals such as deer and rabbits. More than three thousand years ago, they learned how to farm. Growing corn, beans, and squash enabled them to settle into permanent villages.

Over time, they developed into several distinct cultures, including the Anasazi, the Mogollon, the Sinagua, and the Hohokam. Each of these groups created a complex civilization. They sometimes built pueblos—stone buildings, some four stories high—and made artful pottery with dazzling decoration. They grew crops and traded goods with each other and with Indians in Mexico. The Hohokam even dug a vast system of irrigation canals from the Salt River, enabling them to farm in the Sonoran Desert.

One by one between 1200 and 1450, these cultures disappeared. No one is quite sure why. In some cases drought may have been the culprit; in other cases, perhaps disease or warfare. In many places, it looks like the Indians simply walked away from their pueblos, leaving everything behind. Of course all of these people did not simply vanish. The Anasazi are believed to be the ancestors of the Hopi, who live on the high mesas of northeastern Arizona. The Hohokam probably became the modern desert peoples, the Pima and the Tohono O'odham.

During the 1400s, the Navajo and Apache began arriving in the

The Hopi Indians first built pueblos atop mesas in north-western Arizona more than eight hundred years ago.

Southwest from present-day Canada and Alaska. The Navajo settled among the buttes and canyons of northeastern Arizona, where they grew crops and raised sheep. The Apache headed to the mountains farther south. There the men hunted game, and the women gathered nuts and berries.

THE SPANIARDS ARRIVE

By the 1500s, Spain had gained control of Mexico. The Spaniards often heard tales of fantastic cities to the north, cities so wealthy the streets were paved with gold. In 1539, an expedition led by Marcos de Niza set out in search of these fabled cities, called the Seven Cities of Cíbola. Marcos and his companions were likely the first non-Indians to set foot in Arizona.

The following year, a party led by Francisco Vásquez de Coronado trekked through Arizona in search of Cíbola. As Coronado turned east toward New Mexico, one of his men, García López de Cárdenas, headed off to investigate rumors of a great river. When Cárdenas gazed into the Grand Canyon, however, the "great river" at the bottom appeared to be little more than a stream. The Spaniards were looking for riches. To them, the Grand Canyon was nothing but an impassable barrier, so Cárdenas turned around to catch up with the others. Coronado went all the way to present-day Kansas before finally realizing that the legendary cities were, in fact, a legend.

In the coming decades, only a handful of Spanish expeditions passed through Arizona. For Europeans, the region seemed to offer little but unbearable heat. The few who stayed were missionaries seeking to convert the Native Americans to Christianity. In 1629,

Besides founding a string of missions, Father Eusebio Kino was also an important explorer. He was the first European to realize that Baja California was not an island.

missionaries arrived at the Hopi mesas. They forced the Indians to build mission churches, work the land, and learn Spanish culture. They even forbade the Indians to practice their own religion. When the Pueblo Indians in New Mexico rose up against the Spaniards in 1680 and drove them out, the Hopi also rebelled. Although the Spaniards later reconquered northern New Mexico, the missionaries never returned to the Hopi villages.

Missionaries had better luck in southern Arizona, largely because of the efforts of a priest named Eusebio Kino. Father Kino was humble and compassionate. He treated the Pima and Tohono O'odham Indians with kindness and respect. He taught them new farming techniques and how to raise cattle and sheep. Kino eventually established

At missions such as San Xavier del Bac, the Spaniards tried to convert the Indians to Christianity.

twenty-nine missions in northern Mexico and southern Arizona, the farthest north in Bac, near present-day Tucson.

The goodwill Kino established did not survive his death. The missionaries who replaced him treated the Indians cruelly. In 1751, the Indians fought back, killing more than a hundred priests, ranchers, and other settlers. To prevent future uprisings, the Spaniards built a fort at Tubac. This was Arizona's first white settlement.

CHANGING FLAGS

In 1810, Mexico began a long and bloody struggle for independence from Spain. When Mexico finally triumphed in 1821, Arizona was suddenly part of a new country. This made little difference to most people in this remote region. They simply lowered the Spanish flag and raised the Mexican one.

In 1848, most of Arizona changed flags again. The United States had just won in a war with Mexico. As part of the Treaty of Guadalupe Hidalgo that concluded the war, Mexico ceded to the United States a huge swath of land from Texas to California. Arizona was part of the bargain. Six years later, the United States bought the southernmost part of Arizona from Mexico in the Gadsden Purchase.

To Americans, Arizona was an unknown wilderness, nothing but dreaded country that had to be crossed to get to California. The army sent out parties to scout and map the region. In 1869, Major John Wesley Powell, who had lost his right arm during the Civil War, led the first expedition down the Colorado River all the way through the Grand Canyon. For three months, their rafts were buffeted by rapids and battered against rocks. Powell's spellbinding reports alerted the rest of the country to the splendors of the canyon. It wasn't long before tourists started trickling in.

THE INDIAN WARS

As whites began arriving in Arizona, the army set to subduing the Indians, who sometimes raided white settlements. Try as they might, the Indians could not stem the tide of whites taking over their land.

In 1863, Colonel Kit Carson was ordered to round up the Navajo. He took the job seriously, chasing the Indians through the canyons where they lived, burning their crops and destroying their livestock. Facing starvation, the Navajo had no choice but to surrender. Carson then forced them on a three-hundred-mile trek during the dead of winter to a desolate spot in eastern New Mexico called Bosque Redondo. Without adequate food or clothing, hundreds died on what the Navajo call the Long Walk.

Five years later, after thousands more had starved to death at Bosque Redondo, the Navajo were given a reservation in their homeland. Arriving back in Arizona, "we felt like talking to the ground, we loved it so," said Navajo leader Manuelito.

John Wesley Powell's party put their boats in the Green River, which flows into the Colorado, to begin his second expedition through the Grand Canyon.

"I was born on the prairies where the wind blew free and there was nothing to break the light of the sun," Geronimo once said. *"I was born where there were no enclosures."*

Meanwhile, in southern Arizona a bloody war was raging between the U.S. Army and a band of Apache led by Cochise. During eleven years of skirmishes, Cochise never lost a battle. But in 1872, he gave up the fight anyway, agreeing to settle on a reservation.

One by one, the other Arizona tribes surrendered. Finally, only a small band of Apache led by Geronimo remained free. Geronimo's wife and three children had been killed by bounty hunters in 1858.

"I could not call back my loved ones," he later declared, "but I could rejoice in . . . revenge." Geronimo hardened into a great warrior. His pride and determination became legendary. Though there were thousands of troops after them, he and his thirty-eight cohorts managed to hold out until 1886, when they were finally captured and sent to a prison camp in Florida.

THE BIRTH OF PHOENIX

In 1867, a prospector named Jack Swilling was riding through the Salt River valley when he noticed the remnants of the canals that

Jack Swilling, the founder of Phoenix, was also a gold seeker, an all-around adventurer, and perhaps a thief. He died in Yuma Territorial Prison after being accused of robbing a stagecoach.

the Hohokam had dug a thousand years before. Swilling realized that if farms had once covered the desert floor, they could again. He had the ditches rebuilt, irrigated the land, and soon wheat and barley were poking up out of the once arid soil. The town that grew up around the rebuilt canals was named Phoenix, after the mythical bird that dies in a burst of flames and then rises again from the ashes.

Cattle ranching was also rising in Arizona. Between 1870 and 1890, the number of cattle grazing on Arizona's meadows and grasslands leaped from 5,000 to 1.5 million. After the railroads were built in the 1870s and 1880s, Arizona farmers and ranchers were better able to ship their goods to market.

THE WILD WEST

Although some families moved to Arizona to farm and put down roots, many more young men drifted into the territory in search of adventure and a new start in life. They were seeking their fortunes, and they were seeking freedom. In many cases, freedom meant freedom from the law. Pioneer Arizona was rough and lawless. In 1862, army captain John C. Cremony reported that in Tucson, "Men walked the streets with double-barreled shotguns, hunting each other as sportsmen hunt for game. In the graveyard there were 47 graves of white men in 1860, and of that number only 2 had died natural deaths."

Few places were wilder than the mining boomtowns. Gold was discovered along the Gila River in 1858. Almost overnight, two thousand fortune hunters rushed into the area. In less than two years, the gold was tapped out, and the disappointed

The railroads built through Arizona's rugged terrain in the 1880s connected the remote region with the rest of the country.

prospectors moved on to their next dream.

This pattern was repeated again and again. In 1877, Ed Schieffelin struck silver. Almost overnight, the town of Tombstone sprang up. Its streets were filled with gamblers and gunfighters, drinkers and thieves. In Tombstone's violent early days, it was often hard to tell the good guys from the bad guys. One afternoon in 1881, U.S. marshall Wyatt Earp, his brothers Virgil and Morgan, and Doc

THE LOST DUTCHMAN MINE

Arizona's mining days are the stuff of legend. Stories abound about fortunes made—and lost—overnight. One tall tale still looms large in the minds of Arizonans.

People say that back in the 1870s, Jacob Waltz, whom locals called the Dutchman, made a fabulous gold strike in the rugged Superstition Mountains east of Phoenix. Whenever he came to town, he paid for his purchases with gold. Waltz sometimes bragged about the strike, but swore up and down that he would never tell anyone where it was. Folks asked, begged, and threatened, but he never breathed a word. Some say that Waltz killed anyone who followed him into the mountains.

Although Waltz is long gone the legend lives on. To this day, fortune hunters scramble up the Superstitions' peaks and down its ravines, searching for the Lost Dutchman Mine.

Less optimistic souls just think it's a great story. In March, you'll find some of them in Apache Junction for the Lost Dutchman Gold Mine Superstition Mountain Trek. During the daylong festivities, some folks head out on a grueling hike through the mountains. Others prefer to stick behind and eat fresh-baked bread, pan for gold, and enjoy a rousing pageant about the legend of the Lost Dutchman. The night concludes with brilliant fireworks over the dark, craggy hills.

Holliday faced off against Sheriff Johnny Behan and the Clanton clan. Within thirty seconds, three men lay dying and two were wounded, and the gunfight at the O.K. Corral was on its way to becoming American legend. Dozens of movies have been made about that fateful day.

DOWN IN THE MINES

Unlike the silver and gold strikes, copper mining had a lasting impact in Arizona, becoming one of its chief industries. Many people got rich off of copper, but not the men who toiled hundreds of feet underground. There, amid dim light and hot, foul air, they blasted the ore out of the earth. It was dangerous work. Explosions, cave-ins, and fires took many lives.

Eventually, some miners joined unions to try to force the mine owners to improve working conditions. In 1917, miners in Bisbee, the state's leading copper town, went on strike. In response, a group of armed men rounded up the strikers. The more than one thousand strikers who refused to return to work were forced into

In 1917, hundreds of striking miners in Bisbee were herded into boxcars and shipped to New Mexico, where they were dumped in the desert.

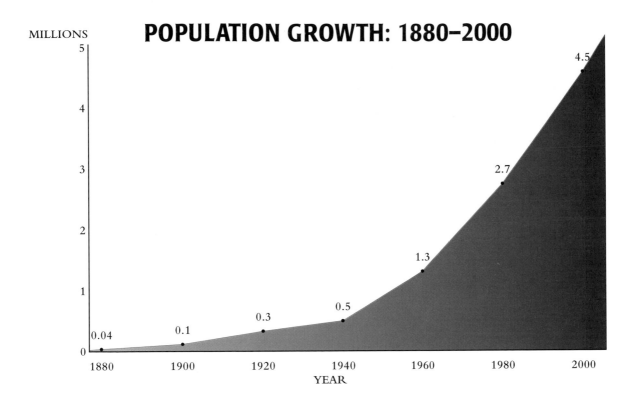

POPULATION GROWTH: 1880–2000

MILLIONS

railroad cars and shipped off to New Mexico, in what is known as the Bisbee Deportation. Few ever returned, and unions never gained much power in Arizona.

INTO THE TWENTIETH CENTURY

By 1910, Arizona was home to more than 200,000 people. Arizonans had long been clamoring for statehood. On Valentine's Day of 1912 they finally got their wish, becoming the forty-eighth state in the Union.

Many Arizonans had also been clamoring for a more dependable supply of water to irrigate their fields. In 1911, the Theodore Roosevelt Dam was completed on the Salt River, and the valley blossomed. In the coming decades, dams would slow rivers across the state, providing Arizonans with water, flood control, and cheap electric power.

Early in the twentieth century, Arizona's fortunes were linked to that of the copper industry. During World War I, demand for copper was high, so prices were high and Arizona prospered. During the Great Depression of the 1930s, copper prices tumbled, and Arizona suffered along with the rest of the nation.

Then, in 1941, the Japanese attacked Pearl Harbor in Hawaii, and the United States entered World War II. Suddenly, Arizona was back in business as the military demanded huge quantities of the state's three most important products—copper, cattle, and cotton. The military also built air bases in Arizona to take advantage of the clear skies.

Not everyone prospered from the war. For some Americans, it brought hardship. All along the West Coast, people of Japanese descent were forced from their homes and into camps out of fear that they might be loyal to Japan. So many Japanese Americans were herded into a camp in Poston, Arizona, that for a time it was the state's third-largest city.

THE BOOM YEARS

With the dams and irrigation projects and the wartime boom, Arizona flourished. But it was air-conditioning that made the state

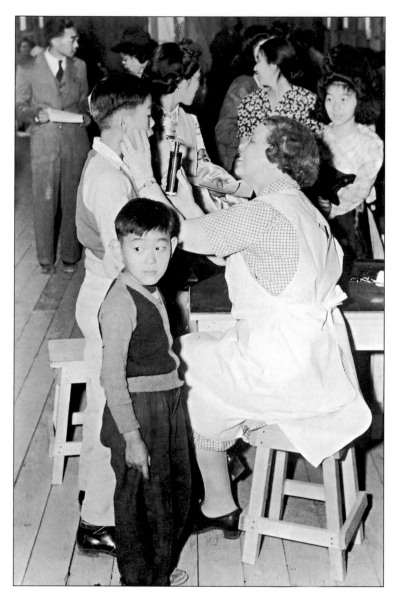

During World War II, thousands of Japanese Americans from the West Coast were forced to live in camps in Arizona.

what it is today. Before air-conditioning was perfected in the 1950s, Phoenix was primarily a winter retreat. Air-conditioning made it livable year-round. In 1950, just 107,000 people lived in Phoenix. By 1960, the city was bursting at the seams with four times that number.

THE NAVAJO CODE TALKERS

It was World War II, and the United States had a problem. The only way for troops to communicate during battle was to radio coded messages, but the Japanese could break the codes as fast as Americans could develop them.

Then someone got the idea of making a code from Navajo, a language so difficult that at the time only about thirty non-Navajo could speak it. So twenty-nine Navajo Marines got together and came up with hundreds of code words for military terms and letters of the alphabet. They memorized them and practiced until they could send and translate messages perfectly.

No one ever broke the Navajo's code. "It sounded like gibberish," said one code expert. "We couldn't even transcribe it, much less crack it." Even other Navajo couldn't make heads or tails of it.

In all, four hundred Navajo became code talkers. Military commanders used them to send orders and warn troops that were in danger of being hit by American fire. They saved countless lives.

Their finest moment came during the battle for the tiny South Pacific island of Iwo Jima. In the first two days of the invasion, six

code talker units worked round the clock, sending eight hundred messages without a single mistake. The Marines finally took control of the island after a month of fierce fighting. It was a turning point in the war. "Were it not for the Navajo code talkers," says Major Howard Conner of the Fifth Marine Division, "the Marines would never have taken Iwo Jima."

The Arizona sunshine beckoned to people in the cold, rainy north. Families, retired folks, and businesses moved south. Houses were built, cities grew in the desert, and canals were constructed to bring water hundreds of miles from the Colorado River to supply their needs.

Today, Arizona remains one of the nation's fastest-growing states, as people continue to flock to where it seems the sun always shines.

3 MAKING LAWS AND LIVINGS

The capitol in Phoenix

Before it became a state, Arizona had to draft a constitution by which it would be governed. When President William Taft saw the document, he was disturbed. The proposed constitution included a clause that allowed voters to recall judges—to remove them from office. Taft, himself a former judge, refused to allow Arizona to become a state until this clause was removed. But Arizonans expect to have a say in their government—and they don't like being pushed around. So in the very first election after Arizona became a state, the recall rule was voted right back in.

INSIDE GOVERNMENT

Like the federal government, the Arizona state government is divided into three branches: executive, legislative, and judicial.

Executive. The head of the executive branch is the governor, who is elected to a four-year term. The governor is responsible for appointing important officials, proposing a state budget, and focusing attention on issues that he or she thinks are important.

In 1998, Arizona voters made U.S. history when they elected women to the state's top five executive branch offices. In addition to Governor Jane Hull, women were also elected secretary of state, attorney general, treasurer, and superintendent of public instruction. During the election, Arizonans paid little attention to the

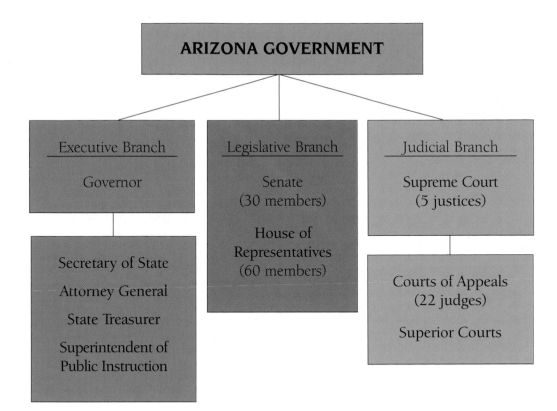

ARIZONA GOVERNMENT

Executive Branch

Governor

Secretary of State

Attorney General

State Treasurer

Superintendent of
Public Instruction

Legislative Branch

Senate
(30 members)

House of
Representatives
(60 members)

Judicial Branch

Supreme Court
(5 justices)

Courts of Appeals
(22 judges)

Superior Courts

gender of the candidates. And even after the four Republicans and one Democrat were elected, the event received little fanfare, which was perfectly alright with these Arizona leaders. "I would hope that people judge me on what I accomplish," says Governor Hull.

Legislative. The Arizona legislature is composed of a thirty-member senate and a sixty-member house of representatives. Both senators and representatives are elected for two-year terms. The legislators make new laws and change old ones. After a proposed law is approved by both houses, it is sent to the governor. The bill becomes law when the governor signs it. The governor can also veto, or reject, the bill. The bill then becomes law only if two-thirds of the members of both houses pass it again.

Judicial. The highest court in Arizona is the state supreme court. Its five justices are appointed by the governor to six-year terms. After that, Arizona voters decide whether or not the justice should remain on the court.

In Arizona, the most serious cases are usually heard in the superior courts in each county. The governor appoints the superior court judges in Maricopa and Pima counties, where Phoenix and Tucson are located. In the other counties, voters elect the judges. If someone thinks a mistake was made in superior court, he or she can ask for the case to be reviewed by the court of appeals. This court has two divisions with a total of twenty-two judges. All are appointed by the governor to six-year terms. Those who are still not satisfied with the ruling can appeal to the supreme court.

WILD WEST POLITICS

Although it has been a long time since the Earp boys strode the wooden sidewalks of Tombstone, public life in Arizona is still wild and woolly. People often have strong opinions. "The politics, it's just like the 1880s," says one woman from Tombstone. "At the city council meetings, people are always yelling and screaming at each other." Things got so rowdy that the city eventually passed a law fining anyone who makes trouble during the meetings. The only way to stay out of trouble, she says, is to keep your opinions to yourself. "People tell me what they think, and I just say 'uh huh, uh huh, uh huh.' But I don't tell them anything. People hate each other. They may not hang people at the cottonwood tree anymore, but they run them out of town."

Barry Goldwater carried just six states in the 1964 presidential election against Lyndon Johnson. "When you've lost an election by that much," he commented, "it isn't the case of whether you made the wrong speech or wore the wrong necktie. It was just the wrong time."

One Arizonan who was never afraid of telling anybody what he thought was Senator Barry Goldwater. In the 1960s, most people believed that the government could make the country a better place. But not Goldwater. He believed in self-reliance. "I have little interest in streamlining government or making it more efficient, for I mean to reduce its size," Goldwater once wrote. "My aim is not to pass laws, but to repeal them." Although he lost the 1964 presidential election in a landslide, his influence has echoed through the years. He is considered the founder of the conservative political movement that has dominated American politics in recent decades.

Like Goldwater, many Arizonans are individualists. They don't like anyone telling them what they can or cannot do. They don't like government regulations. And they don't like taxes.

As a result, the state spends less money on education and programs to help the poor than most other states. Arizona ranks forty-eighth among the fifty states in the number of children with health insurance and near the bottom in how much it spends on each public school student. Some people are hopeful that the state's priorities are changing, since Governor Jane Hull, who was once a teacher, has emphasized education.

Improving education has been on the minds of many Arizonans in recent years.

The issue of bilingual education is at the top of her agenda. About 100,000 Arizona children are in programs for students who speak limited English. While learning English, they are taught other subjects such as math and science in their native Spanish, so they don't fall behind the other students. Some people are unhappy with this approach. "These are expensive programs, and they are not working," says Norma Alvarez, who is fighting bilingual education. "Kids are not learning." Opponents of bilingual education argue that if you put kids in regular classes, they pick up English quickly enough.

Others say this is nonsense. "Children cannot learn if they cannot understand what the teacher is saying," says principal Carlos Bejarano. They also point out that bilingual education allows children to become fluent in both languages, which is a great advantage in today's economy. "We are talking about brains, not car radiators," says Josue Gonzalez, an expert on bilingual education. "You don't have to empty out one language and fill it up with another." And so the argument rages on, with some people trying to increase funding for bilingual education and others trying to eliminate it entirely.

In its drive to save money, Arizona has sometimes been more innovative than other states. Most states have gotten tough on crime in recent years, putting more people in jail for longer periods. But Arizona has found that this isn't the most effective—or the most economical—way of dealing with all problems. Rather than locking up people convicted of nonviolent drug crimes, the state treats their drug problems. Illegal drug users are given counseling and put on probation, so their progress is monitored. The result?

GUACAMOLE

Mexican food is so popular in Arizona that Tucson once proclaimed itself the Mexican Food Capital of the World, apparently forgetting about the nation to the south.

Guacamole is a quick and delicious dish that can be eaten with chips or along with any Mexican food. Have an adult help you with this recipe.

2 soft, ripe avocados
1 chile
1 tomato
2 tablespoons minced onion
juice from ½ lime
½ teaspoon salt

Peel the avocados and remove the pits. Mash the avocado with a fork, leaving some small chunks. (Guacamole should not be smooth.) Slice the chile in half the long way and throw away the seeds. Mince the chile and chop the tomato. Mix these and the onion in with the avocado. Squeeze the lime juice into the mixture. Add salt.

Your guacamole is best if eaten right away, so grab some chips and enjoy.

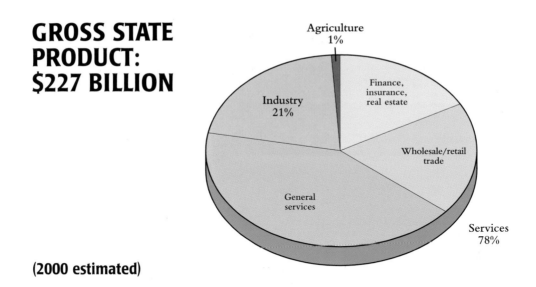

GROSS STATE PRODUCT: $227 BILLION

Agriculture 1%

Industry 21%

Finance, insurance, real estate

Wholesale/retail trade

General services

Services 78%

(2000 estimated)

Nearly 80 percent of the people involved in the program have stayed free of drugs. "Treatment works when it's done right," says Barbara Broderick, the state director of adult probation. Arizona saved $2.5 million in the program's first year because it costs much less to treat people than to imprison them. But, Broderick says, "When we can't get someone to change, we send them to prison. You can't continue to waste resources."

MAKING A LIVING

Arizona's first industry was mining, and it remains important today. Arizona produces more copper than all forty-nine other states combined. Much of it is dug from the ground in giant open-pit mines. The Morenci Mine, in southeastern Arizona, is the second-largest open-pit copper mine in the world. It is an amazing

EARNING A LIVING

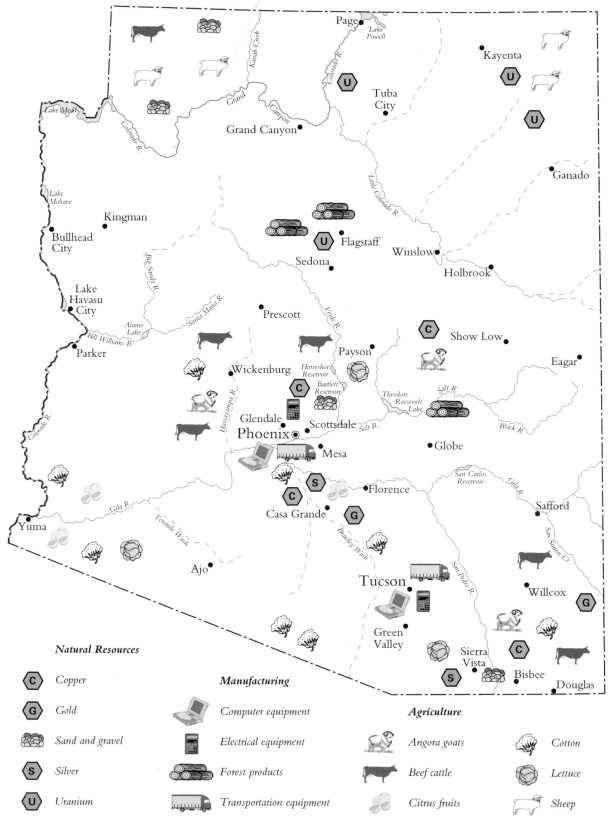

Natural Resources

C — Copper
G — Gold
Sand and gravel
S — Silver
U — Uranium

Manufacturing

Computer equipment
Electrical equipment
Forest products
Transportation equipment

Agriculture

Angora goats
Beef cattle
Citrus fruits
Cotton
Lettuce
Sheep

Mining copper, one of Arizona's leading resources, often leaves vast pits in the earth.

sight: gigantic trucks at the bottom of the gaping chasm look like toy cars. Gold, silver, coal, and sand and gravel are also coaxed from the earth in Arizona.

Although few people think of Arizona as a farm state, many crops are grown there. It is one of the leading cotton-producing states and an important supplier of lettuce, melons, and citrus fruits. Cattle graze over parts of Arizona. Raising sheep is also common, especially on the Navajo Reservation.

Everything from computer chips to spacecraft is produced in Arizona. Here, engineers make a mirror for a telescope.

Most manufacturing in Arizona is concentrated near Phoenix and Tucson. Factories in the region churn out televisions, airplane parts, and even spacecraft. In recent years, more and more Arizonans have been employed producing semiconductors and other computer

The Navajo Indians have a long history of raising sheep in northeastern Arizona.

Millions of people travel to Arizona each year to enjoy the weather and opportunities for outdoor fun.

components. The computer industry also provides a living for people who develop software and design websites. Such high-tech industries are among the fastest-growing segments of the economy.

With its lakes and canyons, golf courses and ghost towns, Arizona has a booming tourist industry. Each year, millions of visitors spend billions of dollars in the state. Although this results in lots of jobs at resorts, restaurants, car rental agencies, and the like, they are usually low paying. Consequently, many Arizonans are just getting

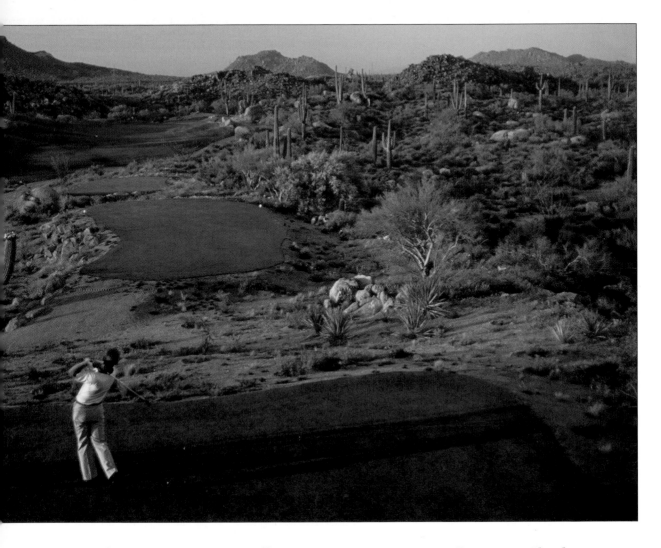

by. "Tucson is generally a minimum-wage town," reports Charles Bowden, who writes about the Southwest.

Many people who arrive in Arizona discover that even for jobs that require more training, wages are lower than they are elsewhere. For instance, after moving to Phoenix a bookkeeper discovered that she would be making just seven dollars an hour instead of thirteen, as she did back in Massachusetts. But for her, the Arizona lifestyle makes it worth it. "You get paid in sunshine," she says.

4 THE GOOD LIFE

So many people have poured into Arizona in recent years that Arizonans sometimes joke that anyone who has been there more than fifteen minutes is a native. But for every person who arrives in Arizona looking to start over, another is already there, trying to hold on to the cherished past.

COMING AND GOING

Arizona's population has been growing by leaps and bounds for decades. The state's population grew nearly 30 percent between 1987 and 1997. Many people come for the weather, others because they see beauty in the harsh landscape. Still others fall for the romance of the West, dreaming of freedom or a new start or a chance to live closer to the land. "I don't like the hustle and bustle of the big city, that's why I came here," says one woman who moved from California to the rugged mountains of southeastern Arizona.

But many of the dreamers are quickly disillusioned. "Anybody from New York moves here, we give them six months," says one Tombstone resident. "Sooner or later, most of them throw up their hands and leave. I mean, there's not even a grocery store here."

People come and go just as much in the Phoenix and Tucson areas, where 85 percent of Arizonans live. For every three people who move into the Phoenix area, two leave. This constant flux can

TEN LARGEST CITIES

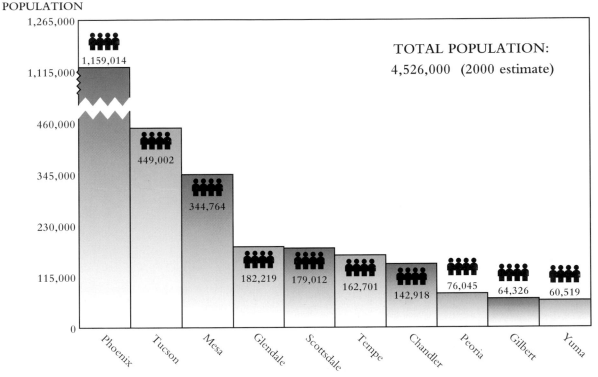

POPULATION

TOTAL POPULATION:
4,526,000 (2000 estimate)

1,265,000
1,159,014
1,115,000
460,000
449,002
345,000
344,764
230,000
182,219 179,012 162,701 142,918
115,000
76,045 64,326 60,519
0

Phoenix Tucson Mesa Glendale Scottsdale Tempe Chandler Peoria Gilbert Yuma

make life difficult for Arizonans. They are less likely to know their neighbors than people elsewhere. It can be particularly hard on children, who keep watching their friends move away. At one Phoenix elementary school, so many families come and go that only one-third of the students stay for more than one year. Some people think all this flux makes Arizonans less involved in their communities. Perhaps that is why Arizona has one of the nation's lowest voter turnout rates.

Other people believe the mobility makes folks more open. "It just makes you more sympathetic to the needs of new people," says one Phoenix resident. "Because so many people who settle here come without friends or family," adds journalist Robert D. Kaplan, "when people do meet they connect quickly."

SNOWBIRDS

Many of the people who have swarmed into Arizona in the last fifty years are elderly. Some are so-called snowbirds, northerners who

With nearly 450,000 residents, Tucson is Arizona's second-largest city.

Most retired folks in Arizona like to stay active. They skate, hike, bike, and bowl. Says Kathy Wenzlau, the director of the fitness center at Sun City Grand, "Someone asked me the other day about the possibility of hang-gliding. We're looking into that."

hop in their mobile homes and head south when the snows come. They enjoy the sunny Arizona winter and then head back north again. When they descend on a quiet Arizona town, it's an amazing sight. In summer, about two thousand people live in the town of Quartzsite near the California border. In winter, Quartzsite's population tops one million. Not everyone stays the whole winter. "RVs suit our lifestyle," says one senior. "We're just active kind of people. After a few weeks we want to move on."

Others buy homes in towns built just for senior citizens. With 45,000 residents, Sun City, west of Phoenix, is the nation's largest retirement community. Places like Sun City are more than just houses. They have swimming pools and golf courses, arts centers and weight rooms. "We're in the fitness center five days a week," says a retired dentist. "We're also learning how to oil paint and doing some pottery. There's enough options to choke a horse." "There's not much retiring going on around here," chortles another elderly woman.

PROUD TRADITIONS

Although many Arizonans are newcomers, many others are from Native American families that have lived there for centuries. Arizona has the third-highest Indian population of any state. The Navajo alone number more than 200,000. Their vast reservation, which spreads from northeastern Arizona into Utah and New Mexico, is larger than West Virginia.

Other Indians in Arizona include Apache, Hopi, Yavapai, Huala-pai, Havasupai, and Tohono O'odham peoples. Many Arizona Indians have tried to maintain some of their tribal traditions. For instance, the Tohono O'odham, who live in the Sonoran Desert, were traditionally masters at gathering food in the seemingly inhospitable land. Over the course of the year, they collected the fruit and seeds of 375 different plants, some of which were only available for a few days. Although many O'odham still live in the desert, today they are much more likely to get their food from supermarkets. But many still use long sticks to pick the fruit that grow atop the saguaro cacti.

Many Indians in Arizona try to maintain their traditions, such as this Apache womanhood ceremony.

They make this fruit into jelly, much as their ancestors did.

Likewise, some Navajo still tend sheep, just as their parents and grandparents did. They pass on to their children the knowledge of how to weave the beautiful rugs for which the Navajo are famous. Of course, many other Navajo have left behind the traditional rural ways for opportunities in the cities. "Our jobs took us away from the sheep," states Betty Reid, a Navajo journalist who lives in Phoenix. "Asphalt, air pollution and the American Dream replaced the wide views, sage-scented air and nomadic ways."

Each September, the Navajo honor the old ways and the new at the Navajo Nation Fair, the world's largest Native American fair. For five days, the town of Window Rock crackles with energy, as Indians and non-Indians alike enjoy rodeos, parades, and exhibits

THE BIRTH OF BUTTERFLIES: A TALE FROM THE TOHONO O'ODHAM

One day the Creator was relaxing, watching a group of children play. As the children cavorted and sang, the Creator grew sad. He realized that one day the children would grow old. Their hair would turn gray and their strength would fail, just as everything eventually withers and dies. Flowers shrivel and leaves fall from trees. The Creator grew even sadder at this thought, for winter was approaching. Soon the cold would set in, and no flowers or leaves would brighten the landscape.

But it was not yet winter. The sun was still shining. The sky was blue, yellow leaves were wafting gently to the ground, women were grinding white corn into meal. Purple and red flowers sprouted here and there. The Creator smiled. "I have to preserve these colors," he thought. "I will make something for the children to enjoy."

So the Creator took his bag and began filling it. He put in a handful of sunlight, some blue from the sky, a bit of white from the corn, some lines of black from a child's hair, yellow from leaves, green from pine needles, purple from flowers.

After putting all the colors he could find in the bag, he gave it to the children, saying, "This is for you. Open it."

When they opened the bag, hundreds of colorful butterflies emerged, flitting and fluttering around the children's heads. Their eyes grew wide and smiles spread across their faces, and the Creator's heart lifted.

ETHNIC ARIZONA

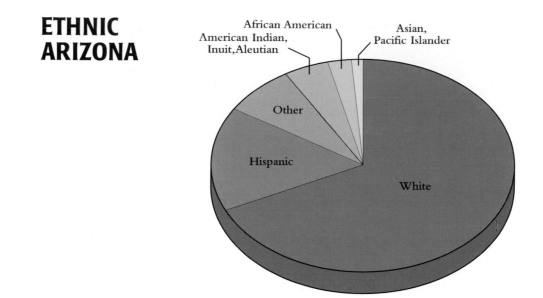

African American

American Indian, Inuit, Aleutian

Asian, Pacific Islander

Other

Hispanic

White

of jewelry, blankets, and other crafts. Some of the most popular events are the traditional dance competitions.

Arizona is home to more than a million Latinos. Like Indians, many of them have roots in Arizona that go all the way back to when it was part of Mexico rather than the United States. "It's so funny when people ask me when my family immigrated to the United States," says Gloria Medina who comes from a family of ranchers near Tucson. "They don't understand that many of us have been here all along." Other Mexicans have arrived more recently, as have Puerto Ricans, Cubans, Nicaraguans, and Guatemalans.

During the nineteenth century, Irish, Germans, Italians, and Serbs came to Arizona to work in the copper mines. Some African Americans also migrated to Arizona to work as cowboys because

LOS VAQUEROS

You'd never know it from all the Hollywood Westerns, but the first cowboys were Mexican. Back before the United States even existed, *vaqueros*, as cowboys are called in Spanish, were riding and roping with astonishing skill.

Many of the English words related to cowboys come from Spanish. *Vaquero* itself became the English *buckaroo*. *La reata* became lariat. *Chaparreras*, the leather leggings worn by cowboys, was shortened to *chaps*. Corral, rodeo, bronco, mustang—they all come from Spanish.

The Hispanic cowboy tradition continued after Arizona became U.S. territory. Many Arizona ranchers and cowboys were Hispanic. The world's first rodeo to award a trophy took place in Prescott, Arizona, in 1888. A man named Juan Leivas won the steer-roping competition and tied for first in bronco riding. This great showing earned him the tournament's Best Cowboy award.

Today, Tucson celebrates its Western past during La Fiesta de los Vaqueros. It features a world-class rodeo and a massive parade of horses, floats, and traditional Mexican musicians and dancers.

the Wild West offered them more freedom than the Old South.

Many Asian immigrants have also made their homes in Arizona. Chinese people began moving to Arizona during pioneer times to build the railroads and work the mines. Some settled in towns such as Prescott and Phoenix, establishing laundries and other small businesses. The twentieth century has seen the arrival of Japanese, Koreans, Vietnamese, and Laotians. In 1946, Phoenix lawyer Wing F. Ong, who had immigrated from China as a teenager, became the first Asian American in the country to win elective office when he won a seat in the Arizona House of Representatives.

Arizonans celebrate their rich heritage in events throughout the year. On September 16, Mexican Independence Day, towns across the state hold festivals to commemorate the first day of Mexico's fight for independence from Spain. These colorful parties echo with mariachi music and fireworks. Many children take to the stage for the Mexican hat dance, dancing around a giant sombrero. Phoenix honors Japanese culture with a festival called Matsuri, where you can see demonstrations of everything from origami to martial arts. Arizona's wild past is remembered at events such as Gold Rush Days in Wickenburg, where folks can pan for gold and enjoy a rodeo.

THE ACTIVE LIFE

Newcomers and old-timers, seniors and teens—it seems everyone in Arizona loves the great outdoors. Skiing, rock climbing, and

Mexican Americans honor their heritage at festivals throughout the year.

bicycling all have their enthusiasts. Golf is another favorite. Each year 11 million rounds of golf are played on the Phoenix area's 187 golf courses.

Although Phoenix gets just seven inches of rain a year (the area is known as the Valley of the Sun), it abounds with pools, fountains, and artificial lakes. Some people question whether this is a wise way to live in a desert. They wonder how long the dams and canals and pumps can keep the booming area supplied with water. But most simply enjoy it. "If you're in the desert, you want an oasis," says one valley resident. Whether swimming, boating, or waterskiing, Arizonans take full advantage of all that water. "I fish year-round, and I'm on the lakes year-round," boasts one. For many, it was this lifestyle that drew them to Arizona. As one Phoenix man says, it's "no-brain, no-hassle living."

A rock climber on Mount Lemmon near Tucson is rewarded with a spectacular view.

5 ARIZONA ORIGINALS

Arizonans are an independent bunch. From art to politics to science, they have never hesitated to go their own way and forge new ground.

MAKING A DIFFERENCE

One of Arizona's greatest sons, Cesar Chavez, devoted his life to helping farm workers who spent long, backbreaking days picking fruits and vegetables for paltry wages.

Chavez was born in 1927 in the arid hills near Yuma, Arizona. His grandparents had a farm, and his father owned a store. When the Great Depression hit, they lost both the land and the business. Like many other families during those hard years, the Chavezes packed up and headed to California. This began their life as migrant farm workers. The family traveled from place to place, following the ripening fruits and vegetables. Moving constantly, the children were in and out of school. Often, they did not attend school at all because the parents earned such pitiful wages that the children were needed to help in the fields. After Cesar completed the eighth grade, he went to work full-time.

As an adult, Chavez never forgot those difficult times. He established a union to try to improve the conditions that kept farm workers in poverty. In 1965, Chavez's union went on strike against

"You are never strong enough that you don't need help," labor organizer Cesar Chavez once said.

California grape growers. Workers in the grape fields often earned only a dollar an hour. Even when they were toiling in 100-degree heat, the growers charged them for drinking water. To draw attention to their demands, Chavez organized a boycott of grapes. All across the nation and even the world, people refused to buy California grapes. It took years, but the grape growers finally settled with the United Farm Workers Organizing Committee. Never before had California farmers signed contracts with a farm workers' union.

After this victory, Chavez continued his fight both in California and in his home state. By 1984, wages for union farm workers had increased to a minimum of seven dollars an hour. Until his death in 1993, Chavez never wavered in his efforts to make life better for farm workers.

BREAKING BARRIERS

It's a long way from the dusty hills of southeastern Arizona to the marble halls of the Supreme Court Building in Washington, D.C. But with her sharp intellect and lots of hard work, Sandra Day

In 1981, Sandra Day O'Connor became the first female justice in the Supreme Court's 191-year history.

O'Connor made the trip and became the first woman to serve on the Supreme Court.

O'Connor spent much of her childhood living in a house without electricity or running water on her family's Lazy B Ranch near Duncan. A child of the West, she learned to ride horses and brand cattle. "I didn't do all the things boys did," O'Connor once said, "but I fixed windmills and repaired fences."

In the coming years, O'Connor found that she could do many other things that boys did. In 1952, she became a lawyer. At the time, few women were lawyers. Although she had finished third in her class at the prestigious Stanford Law School, no law firm would hire her. The only position she was offered was as a legal secretary.

But O'Connor didn't let this stop her. She eventually became an assistant attorney general in Phoenix and then an Arizona state senator. By 1972, her careful approach to lawmaking had so impressed her colleagues that they elected her majority leader of the state senate. She was the first woman to hold this post in any state.

With her fairness and diligence, O'Connor was a natural to become a judge. She was serving on the Arizona Court of Appeals in 1981 when President Ronald Reagan appointed her the U.S. Supreme Court's first female justice. In the years since, O'Connor has proven herself an independent thinker, sometimes siding with the more conservative justices, sometimes with the more liberal ones. No matter how she rules on a case, no one ever doubts that she has given it her full and serious attention. In the end, this is how she wants to be remembered. O'Connor once said she hopes her tombstone reads, "Here lies a good judge."

LOOKING UP

Some people move to Arizona to start over. Others are drawn to the desert landscape. But a few have moved there to look at the sky. In 1894, astronomer Percival Lowell traveled to Arizona because he thought it would be an ideal place to study the planet Mars. At a spot outside Flagstaff, far from the lights and pollution of cities, Lowell set up his telescope.

Lowell spent years studying Mars, concluding, incorrectly as it turned out, that it was home to plant life, water, and even intelligent life. Some of Lowell's other findings proved more accurate, such as his calculation of how long Uranus takes to rotate.

During Lowell's time, scientists knew of only eight planets circling the sun. But Lowell believed there was another one, far beyond Neptune. He spent the last eight years of his life looking for the elusive planet. He never found it, but in 1930, fourteen years after his death, an astronomer at the Lowell Observatory named Clyde Tombaugh discovered the ninth planet. He announced his discovery of Pluto on the seventy-fifth anniversary of Lowell's birth.

ARIZONA VISIONS

Some Arizona artists have been inspired by the state's dramatic landscapes or rich history. Steven Spielberg, the most popular filmmaker of all time, was inspired by its orderly suburbs. When Spielberg was nine, his family moved from New Jersey to Scottsdale, just outside of Phoenix. Spielberg was rather bored by his quiet neighborhood, and he turned to movies for excitement and adventure. By age twelve,

Percival Lowell (third from the right) first set up telescopes in Arizona in 1894.

he had started making his own movies. Spielberg later explained that he had discovered he "could do anything or live anywhere via my imagination, through film."

Steven Spielberg directed three of the top ten money makers in movie history.

Indeed, in making such blockbusters as *Jurassic Park* and *Raiders of the Lost Ark*, Spielberg could cavort with dinosaurs or explore crowded marketplaces in North Africa. But in some of his most personal films, he returned to more familiar surroundings. *E.T., the Extra-Terrestrial*, a movie about a lonely boy who befriends an alien who has been left behind by his spaceship, takes place in a neighborhood just like Scottsdale.

Another prominent Arizona artist, R. C. Gorman, was born far from Scottsdale's tidy streets. Gorman grew up on the sprawling Navajo Reservation. From the time he could hold a pencil, he started drawing. If he didn't have a pencil, he would use a stick to draw pictures in the dirt. It wasn't long before everyone realized he was bursting with talent. At school, Gorman pored over every art book. He was amazed at the incredible variety of paintings made by artists from all over the world. As an adult, he traveled frequently, studying other people's paintings and incorporating their methods into his own work.

Although Gorman painted Native Americans, he did not use the traditional flat, colorful style of Indian paintings. His paintings were modern and expressive, with simple fluid lines. Sometimes he was criticized for moving away from tradition, but by the early 1960s, his

R. C. Gorman was the first person to a have a one-man show at the Museum of the American Indian.

A FRONTIER POET

Many writers have found inspiration in Arizona's mountains and deserts. One of the first was Sharlot Hall, whose family moved from Kansas to Arizona in 1881, when she was eleven years old. The Halls settled in Lonesome Valley, a place Sharlot later recalled was "as bare and brown and lonesome as its name implies—and as beautiful as only the southwestern plains can be."

Each morning, Sharlot and her brother walked four miles to a little school. As she wrote in her poem "Wild Morning Glories" forty years later, they often lingered, admiring the hardy plants that emerged from the islands of earth between rocks.

> Once in a wind-swept, sunburned land
> Where long, rough hills come crawling down,
> Crowding the little valley hard
> With buttes like paws, rock-clawed and brown,
> One great split boulder in the sand
> Made spots of shade where wild vines grew,
> All hung with swinging bells of bloom—
> In sunset colors pink and blue.
> Small morning glory vines that clung
> Back in the rock rifts dim and cool—
> And two ranch children all through May
> Were tardy every day at school.

reputation was growing. Today, he is among the country's leading Native American artists.

Over the years, Gorman's drawings, paintings, and sculptures have had a great influence on young Indian artists. He opened the door for them to explore less traditional forms. "I'm lucky that I can paint what I wish," Gorman once said, "and that people relate to my work in a very personal way."

DESERT DEFENDER

In 1946, nineteen-year-old Edward Abbey hitchhiked west from Pennsylvania, where he had grown up. When he got to the desert, he knew he had found home. He eventually settled in Oracle, Arizona, and spent the rest of his life writing about the Southwest. Abbey's books are rude and funny and angry. One of his best is *Desert Solitaire*, a series of essays about working as a park ranger. Its publication in 1968 spurred on the young environmental movement.

Abbey loved the desert. He reveled in its harsh and dangerous landscape and hated anyone who would harm it—or tame it. To Abbey, the way to experience the wilderness was on its terms, not yours. "No more cars in national parks," he proclaimed. "Let the people walk. Or ride horses, bicycles, mules, wild pigs—anything—but keep the automobiles and motorcycles and all their motorized relatives out."

In one book, he tried to explain why he loves the desert so much. He told of hiking out of a remote canyon and finding an arrow made of rocks, an arrow that had probably been there for a hundred years. It seemed to point at nothing in particular.

> I studied the scene with care, looking for an ancient Indian ruin, a significant cairn, perhaps an abandoned mine, a hidden treasure. . . .
> But there was nothing out there. Nothing at all. Nothing but the desert. Nothing but the silent world.
> *That's why.*

6 WILD AND WONDERFUL

Arizona is a big state with big attractions. No quick tour can hit them all, but here are some highlights.

WILD WEST COUNTRY

"All you'll find will be your tombstone," someone warned prospector Ed Schieffelin when he headed to Apache country in 1877. Instead, he found one of Arizona's richest veins of silver. Within three years, 10,000 people crowded into the brown hills near Tombstone, as Schieffelin had named the town that sprouted around the mines. A decade later, the mines were petering out, and the population had dropped to fewer than two thousand.

Today, with its wooden sidewalks and restored saloons, Tombstone holds tight to its history. Although visitors can watch reenactments of the gunfight at the O.K. Corral, the best way to get a sense of what life was like back in the rough-and-tumble boomtown days is to visit the Boot Hill Graveyard. There you can read the matter-of-fact tombstones recording who was hanged and who was stabbed. With suitable dark humor, one reads, "Here lies Lester Moore. Four slugs from a 44. No Les no more."

Not far from Tombstone is Bisbee, another mining boomtown. A huge supply of copper once lay beneath Bisbee's steep hills and gulches. So many people were busy digging copper out of the

The grave markers in Boot Hill Cemetery are a vivid reminder of Tombstone's violent past.

ground that in 1900 Bisbee was the largest town in Arizona. Today, mining is history in Bisbee, but the town itself is pleasant and picturesque. Many buildings from Bisbee's heyday remain, clinging precariously to the hillsides.

Touring the Copper Queen Mine, where eight billion pounds of copper were taken from the ground over the course of a century,

PLACES TO SEE

Page
Lake Powell
Monument Valley
Kayenta
Grand Canyon
Tuba City
Canyon de Chelly
Kanab Creek
Colorado R.
Grand Canyon
Grand Canyon
Navajo and Hopi Reservations
Ganado
Little Colorado R.
Hoover Dam
Lake Mead
Colorado R.
Wupatki National Monument
Museum of Northern Arizona
Lake Mohave
Kingman
Lowell Observatory
▲ *Humphrey's Peak (12,633 ft.)*
Flagstaff
Winslow
Petrified Forest National Park
Bullhead City
Holbrook
Slide Rock State Park
Sedona
Lake Havasu City
Big Sandy R.
Santa Maria R.
Sharlot Hall Museum
Prescott
Verde R.
Show Low
Alamo Lake
Bill Williams R.
Payson
Eagar
Parker
Wickenburg
Horseshoe Reservoir
Bartlett Reservoir
Theodore Roosevelt Lake
Salt R.
Black R.
Hi Jolly Monument
Hassayampa R.
Salt R.
Scottsdale
Phoenix
Taliesin West
Globe
Mesa
San Carlos Reservoir
Gila R.
Heard Museum
Florence
Safford
Colorado R.
Gila R.
Casa Grande
San Simon Cr.
Yuma
Tenmile Wash
Bradley Wash
San Pedro R.
Saguaro National Park
Chiricahua National Monument
Ajo
Willcox
Organ Pipe Cactus National Monument
Tucson
Arizona-Sonora Desert Museum
Mission San Xavier del Bac
Green Valley
R.I.P. **Tombstone**
Copper Queen Mine
Bisbee
Douglas

is a fun way to learn about Bisbee's mining past. After getting hard hats and yellow rain slickers, visitors climb aboard a mining car and head deep into the earth. The tours are led by real miners, who speak enthusiastically about their profession. "I love the smell of powder," says one after explaining methods of blasting. You'll learn lots of fascinating details on these tours, such as what animals were used to haul equipment underground. "They used mules," says the guide. "Don't talk to me about horses and ponies. They're too stupid. They don't duck if there's a low bridge. They bang their heads to pieces."

Southeastern Arizona also has a wealth of natural wonders. In Texas Canyon, huge boulders are piled atop one another, looking as if they will tumble down at any moment. For an even more amazing sight, head to Chiracahua National Monument, where there are whole forests of giant rock columns. On the park's many hiking trails, you can walk among the towering rocks, through huge archways, and past gigantic rocks improbably balanced on top of columns. You'll also pass some extraordinary plants, such as the alligator juniper, which has bark that cracks into little squares that looks like alligator skin as it spirals its way up the tree trunk.

THE SONORAN DESERT

Lying along the Mexican border in the western part of the state, Organ Pipe Cactus National Monument is a long way from anything. But for beautiful, unspoiled Sonoran Desert, it's hard to beat. The monument gets its name from the organ pipe cactus, which grows only in this part of Arizona. You can see these desert giants,

The Chiracahua Apaches called the region that is now Chiracahua National Monument the "Land of the Standing-Up Rocks."

which have many large stalks shooting up from a single base, and a huge variety of other desert plants on hikes or bumpy drives through the rocky landscape.

Although Tucson is a sprawling city, two of its best stops are dedicated to southern Arizona's extraordinary environment. You can

Although common in northern Mexico, the organ pipe cactus grows in only a small part of southern Arizona.

bike, hike, or drive through beautiful stands of cacti at Saguaro National Park. Although the park is home to a host of animals, you're unlikely to see many besides birds. Most venture out only at night, when the heat wanes. For a close-up view of some of these desert animals, head to the Arizona-Sonora Desert Museum. There you can say hello to tarantulas and scorpions, Gila monsters and mountain lions. You'll also get a good look at the amazing variety of cacti, wildflowers, and other plants that thrive in the Sonoran Desert.

Just south of Tucson is one of the most remarkable remnants of Spanish settlement in Arizona. Mission San Xavier del Bac is an ornate building, filled with scrolls and spires and statues. The mission was completed in 1797. At the time, no building within a thousand miles was as elaborate or ambitious. Today, it is still a strange sight in the Arizona desert.

Phoenix's one must-see site is the Heard Museum, the world's premiere museum of the southwestern Indians. You'll see intricately woven baskets, delicate pottery, and an amazing collection of Hopi kachina dolls. But the Heard is not just about the artifacts of Indian history. It is also about the lifeways and cultures of Native Americans, past and present. So you can walk into a cozy hogan, an eight-sided wooden building in which Navajo traditionally lived, or listen to tapes of Apache, Tohono O'odham, and others talking about their lives.

HEADING WEST

Driving west out of the Valley of the Sun, you'll eventually come to Quartzsite, a rather nondescript town. The best reason to stop there is to see the Hi Jolly monument. In the 1850s, the U.S. Army was trying to improve transportation across the desert Southwest. One experiment involved bringing eighty camels and several camel drivers over from the Middle East. When the experiment fell apart, all the drivers but one returned home. Hadji Ali, whose name was pronounced "Hi Jolly" by the locals, stayed behind. After his death, Hi Jolly was buried in a local cemetery under a huge pyramid with a camel on top, certainly one of Arizona's strangest sights.

Heading north, you gradually make your way into the brown, desolate hills of the Mohave Desert. Eventually, coming over the summit of a particularly steep hill, you can't help but be awed by

San Xavier del Bac is the grandest of the Spanish missions built in the eighteenth century in what is now Arizona.

LONDON BRIDGE

A logical person might assume the London Bridge is in England. But Arizona is, after all, a place where lush lawns carpet the desert floor. Arizona isn't about logic; it's about dreams.

In 1964, Robert McCulloch was looking for a place to build a chainsaw factory. While flying across western Arizona, he spotted Lake Havasu. McCulloch decided the lake was the ideal place for his new town. But how to make Lake Havasu City different from all the other towns sprouting in the Arizona desert?

When McCulloch heard that London was selling its famed bridge, he had his answer. The bridge, built in 1824, could no longer handle the bustling city's traffic. McCullough bought it for $2.5 million. It was taken apart into 10,276 pieces and put back together again, halfway around the world.

But having a bridge span nothing but sun-baked earth seemed rather silly, so a channel was dug beneath it. And what good is a beautiful English bridge that doesn't lead to anything? So up went shops designed in an old English style.

So now the London Bridge crosses an artificial river to a fake English village near a manmade lake. "It's fantastic what you Americans can do," an English visitor once said. "Where you don't have any history, you just make it."

the massive structure in front of you. Hoover Dam is gigantic, as tall as a seventy-story building and two football fields thick. The amount of concrete used to build it could have made a two-lane highway from New York City to San Francisco, California. You'll learn lots of other facts about its construction on a tour of its depths.

CENTRAL ARIZONA

Flagstaff, the largest city in central Arizona, makes an excellent base for exploring the region's wealth of natural and historical wonders. But before you head out of town, stop by a couple of Flagstaff's sights that shouldn't be missed. At Lowell Observatory, you can learn what astronomers do, find out more about the galaxy with hands-on exhibits, and get a close-up view of the telescope Clyde Tombaugh used when he discovered the planet Pluto in 1930. On some evenings the observatory allows visitors to look through one of its large telescopes. Nearby, the Museum of Northern Arizona is filled with fascinating exhibits about everything from how the Grand Canyon was created to how Anasazi pottery changed over the centuries.

North of Flagstaff is Wupatki National Monument, where the ruins of several magnificent pueblos built by the Sinagua during the 1100s dot the desolate landscape. The largest of these, called the Wupatki Pueblo, was once three stories tall and contained a hundred rooms. Although the Sinagua abandoned Wupatki around 1225, some of their magnificent stonework is still intact.

Driving south from Flagstaff into the red rock country near Sedona will make your jaw drop. From the blinding red rock cliffs to the deep green pine forests to the glistening waters of Oak Creek, it is a magical place. Add a dusting of bright white snow and the colors are phenomenal. The red rock country can be enjoyed in many ways. Just driving some of its spectacular roads will bring gasps at the glorious scenery. Hikers have their choice of a huge

"I wouldn't live anywhere else," says one well-traveled artist who makes her home in the red rock country near Sedona.

array of trails that head down refreshing creeks and past stunning formations such as Cathedral Rock or Devil's Bridge. During summer, nothing can beat a trip down the natural rock slides into the swimming hole at Slide Rock State Park.

Farther south lies Prescott. Once the territorial capital, today it retains much of its early charm. Prescott is home to the Sharlot Hall Museum, which was named for the poet who grew up nearby. When Hall was appointed territorial historian in 1909, she became the first woman to hold public office in Arizona. Hall's collection of historical artifacts and documents was eventually put on display in the Old Governor's Mansion, a log cabin built in 1864 as a home for the first territorial governor. Today, several buildings make up the Sharlot Hall Museum. The Transportation Building is especially fun, with its old-fashioned high-wheeled bicycle and lavish stagecoach. And don't miss Fort Misery. Within a few years of being built in 1863, this tiny two-room log structure served as the territory's first law office, first Protestant house of worship, first boardinghouse, and first courtroom.

INDIAN COUNTRY

Northeastern Arizona is Indian country. Most of the region belongs to the huge Navajo and Hopi Reservations.

On the edge of the Navajo Reservation is Petrified Forest National Park. Once, huge trees blanketed this region. Eventually these trees fell, and the logs became buried under dirt and volcanic ash. Water carrying minerals seeped into the logs. The water continued on, but the minerals stayed, attaching to the wood tissue. Over time, the minerals built up until the trees had turned to stone filled with colorful crystal patterns.

When tourism first sprang up in Arizona in the late 1800s, visitors carted away as much of this beautiful petrified wood as they could carry. "We had filled our hats with chips," wrote one visitor. "Oh such a time as we did have deciding which part of the forest to leave and which part to pack out." Indeed, so many people packed pieces out—and carted off tons of huge logs on wagons or trains—that much of the forest was lost. Luckily, the area was eventually protected, and today visitors can walk among some of these mind-boggling petrified trees.

The barren pastel hills of the Painted Desert cover much of Petrified Forest National Park. The desert's reds, browns, purples, and blues come from the varying mineral content in each stripe of rock. The effect is particularly mesmerizing when the sun is low in the sky.

For hundreds of years, the Hopi Indians have made their homes atop three craggy mesas in what is now Arizona's northwestern corner. Walpi village has what is probably the most striking location of any settlement in Arizona. Sitting at the tip of one of these mesas, Walpi floats six hundred feet above the empty surrounding plain. At one point, the mesa narrows to just fifteen feet across. Being there, you get the sensation of living in the sky, surrounded by nothing but the wind. Today, only thirty people live in the dusty village, which has neither electricity nor water, but it remains an important ceremonial site.

East of the Hopi mesas is Canyon de Chelly (pronounced d'SHAY), which many people consider Arizona's prettiest canyon. Its sheer cliffs often appear crumbling and delicate, and they are

Wind and water are constantly washing away the soft, crumbling soil in the Painted Desert, exposing more and more petrified logs.

adorned with streaks that seem to drip down the reddish brown walls. To tour the canyon, visitors can climb into the back of a big blue open-bed truck, which takes them on a wild, bouncing ride along the canyon bottom right through the river that sometimes flows there. The trip takes you past soaring rock formations, ancient Anasazi dwellings tucked into the cliffs, and even hogans where Navajo still live.

For sheer weirdness, few places can match Monument Valley. Its bright red buttes rise from the arid landscape like some other-worldly city. A trip by car on the scenic drive amongst the spires provides amazing vistas, but nothing can beat saddling up a horse and riding close to the monuments. Kicking up the dust, you'll feel like you're in your own private Western.

Driving west out of the Navajo Nation, be sure to stop at the Little Colorado River Canyon. From a distance, it looks like a jagged scar running across the flat grasslands. Up close, you can see that it is a slim canyon with sheer cliffs that drop to the trickle of water far below.

TO THE CANYON

Let's end our tour at the one spot that virtually every tourist to Arizona visits. More than five million people travel to the Grand Canyon every year. Most just spend a few hours there. They check out the viewpoints, peek over the edge, take some photographs, watch the sunset.

But this is not the best way to experience the canyon. To really appreciate it, you have to get down into it. Hike down one of the trails, so you can feel yourself dwarfed by the cliffs and pillars. Another option is to experience the Grand Canyon from the bottom. Some outfits offer mule rides down, and each year, 20,000 people take boats down the Colorado River through the canyon. If you want to get away from all those people, check out edenlike

The White House ruins on the floor of Canyon de Chelly are around nine hundred years old.

Havasu Canyon, a side canyon to the Grand Canyon. Havasu Creek forms spectacular waterfalls as it rushes over red cliffs into blue-green pools far below.

No matter how you experience the Grand Canyon, it is worth the trip. It is, as President Theodore Roosevelt said when he visited the site in 1903, "the one great sight which every American should see."

"It's like the rest of the world has disappeared," said one amazed visitor to the remote and peaceful Havasu Canyon.

THE FLAG: In the center of the Arizona flag is a copper-colored star, which represents the state's most important mineral. From this star radiate rays of yellow and red, the colors of Spain, which once controlled the region. The flag was adopted in 1917.

THE SEAL: Adopted in 1912, Arizona's state seal has images of mining, farming, and cattle ranching, which were once the state's most important economic activites. Above the scene is the state motto, Ditat Deus, which is Latin for "God Enriches."

STATE SURVEY

Statehood: February 14, 1912

Origin of Name: From the Tohono O'odham Indian word *arizonac*, which may mean "small spring"

Nickname: Grand Canyon State

Capital: Phoenix

Motto: God Enriches

Bird: Cactus wren

Flower: Saguaro cactus blossom

Tree: Paloverde

Cactus wren

Saguaro cactus blossom

ARIZONA MARCH SONG

"Arizona March Song" was adopted by the legislature as the official state anthem on February 28, 1919.

Words by
Margaret Rowe Clifford

Music by
Maurice Blumenthal

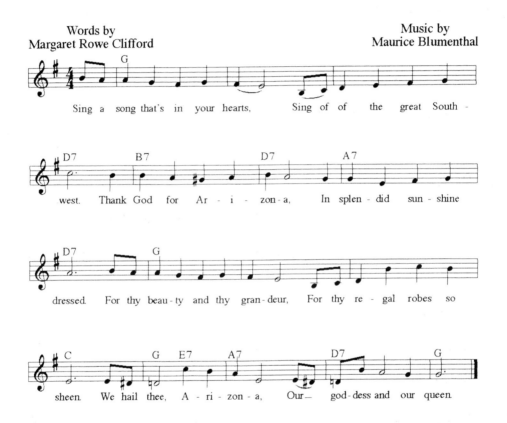

Mammal: Ring-tailed cat

Reptile: Ridge-nosed rattlesnake

Gemstone: Turquoise

Neckwear: Bola tie

Fossil: Petrified wood

Fish: Arizona trout

Amphibian: Arizona tree frog

GEOGRAPHY

Highest Point: 12,633 feet above sea level, at Humphreys Peak

Lowest Point: 70 feet above sea level, along the Colorado River in Yuma County

Area: 114,007 square miles

Greatest Distance, North to South: 389 miles

Greatest Distance, East to West: 337 miles

Bordering States: California and Nevada to the west, Utah to the north, New Mexico to the east

Hottest Recorded Temperature: 127°F in Parker on July 7, 1905

Coldest Recorded Temperature: -40°F at Hawley Lake on January 7, 1971

Average Annual Precipitation: 13 inches

Major Rivers: Bill Williams, Colorado, Gila, Little Colorado, Salt, San Pedro

Major Lakes: Apache, Havasu, Mead, Powell, Theodore Roosevelt, San Carlos

Trees: Arizona oak, blue spruce, cottonwood, Douglas fir, juniper, piñon pine, ponderosa pine, quaking aspen, white fir

Wild Plants: cholla, columbine, creosote, manzanita, ocotillo, phlox, prickly pear, saguaro, sand verbena, yucca

Animals: badger, beaver, black bear, bobcat, Gila monster, javelina, mountain lion, mountain sheep, mule deer, porcupine, pronghorn, raccoon, rattlesnake, red fox, scorpion, tarantula

Birds: cactus wren, dove, eagle, Gila woodpecker, grouse, hawk, hummingbird, nuthatch, purple martin, quail, roadrunner, Stellar's jay, warbler, wild turkey

Fish: bass, bluegill, catfish, crappie, trout, walleye

Endangered Animals: American peregrine falcon, bonytail chub, cactus ferruginous pygmy owl, Colorado squawfish, desert pupfish, Gila topminnow, Gila trout, Hualapai Mexican vole, humpback chub, jaguar, Kanab Ambersnail, lesser bat, masked bobwhite, Mount Graham red squirrel, ocelot, razorback sucker, Sinaloan jaguarundi, Sonoran pronghorn, Sonoran tiger salamander, Southwestern willow flycatcher, Virgin River chub, woundfin, Yaqui chub, Yuma clapper rail

Ocelot

Endangered Plants: Arizona agave, Arizona cliffrose, Arizona hedgehog cactus, Brady pincushion cactus, Canelo Hills ladies'-tresses, Huachuca water-umbel, Kearney's blue-star, Nichol's Turk's head cactus, Peebles Navajo cactus, Pima pineapple cactus, Sentry milk-vetch

TIMELINE

Arizona History

c.1000 Hohokam, Anasazi, Mogollon, Sinagua, and other early Indian groups begin building complex pueblos in present-day Arizona

1200–1450 These cultures disappear

1400s The Navajo and Apache migrate into what is now Arizona; Hopi, Pima, Havasupai, Tohono O'Odham, and other groups also live in the region

1539 Marcos de Niza becomes the first European to set foot in present-day Arizona when he crosses it searching for the Seven Cities of Cíbola

1540 Francisco Vásquez de Coronado visits the Hopi while crossing Arizona

1629 Franciscan priests establish a mission among the Hopi

1687 Eusebio Kino begins missionary work among the Pima

1752 Arizona's first European settlement is established at Tubac

1776 Tucson is founded

1821 Arizona becomes Mexican territory after Mexico gains its independence from Spain

1848 Most of Arizona becomes U.S. territory at the end of the Mexican War

1853 With the Gadsden Purchase, the U.S. takes possession of southern Arizona

1858 Gold is discovered along the Gila River

1859 The *Weekly Arizonan*, Arizona's first newspaper, begins publication in Tubac

1863 Arizona Territory is created

1869 John Wesley Powell leads the first expedition down the entire length of the Grand Canyon

1871 Arizona's first public school opens in Tucson

1877 The Southern Pacific Railroad enters Arizona

1881 The gunfight at the O.K. Corral takes place in Tombstone

1886 Apache warrior Geronimo surrenders

1912 Arizona becomes the 48th state

1936 Hoover Dam is completed

1948 Indians in Arizona receive the right to vote

1965 Lorna Lockwood becomes chief justice of the Arizona Supreme Court, making her the first woman to head a state supreme court

1975 Raul H. Castro becomes Arizona's first Mexican-American governor

1981 Arizonan Sandra Day O'Connor becomes the first woman to serve on the U.S. Supreme Court

ECONOMY

Agricultural Products: barley, beef cattle, broccoli, cauliflower, cotton, dairy products, hay, lemons, lettuce, oranges, sheep, wheat

Cultivating cotton

Manufactured Products: aircraft parts, food products, newspapers, radios, scientific instruments, semiconductors, space vehicles

Natural Resources: copper, crushed stone, gold, sand and gravel, silver

Business and Trade: finance, real estate, tourism, wholesale and retail trade

CALENDAR OF CELEBRATIONS

Winterfest Skiing, snowmobiling, snowshoeing, sled dog races, sleigh rides, historic walking tours—there's something for everyone at this snowy festival in Flagstaff each February.

Matsuri, Festival of Japan Each February, Japanese-Americans in Phoenix honor their past with demonstrations of tea ceremonies, martial arts, sword dancing, and other activities. Visitors can also eat their fill of foods such as sushi (raw fish) and yaki soba (fried noodles).

Wickenberg Gold Rush Days Travel back to the Wild West at this February celebration in Wickenberg. You can learn how to pan for gold, watch the bucking broncos at a rodeo, and check out a mineral show.

La Fiesta de Los Vaqueros The world's largest nonmotorized parade—the floats are pulled by horses—kicks off this February rodeo in Tucson.

Heard Museum Guild Indian Fair & Market Each March, the Heard Museum in Phoenix hosts the Southwest's premiere Indian cultural festival. On display is a huge variety of paintings, ceramics, and other arts. Visitors can also taste such specialties as acorn soup, an Apache dish.

International Mariachi Conference For four days each April, Tucson is filled with the best mariachi music anywhere.

Rendezvous Days The lives of the mountain men—trappers and guides who lived in Arizona in the early 19th century—are remembered at this May celebration in Williams. Festivities include covered wagon rides, parades, dances, and a steak fry.

Prescott Frontier Days and Rodeo Each July, Prescott proudly kicks up its heels at one of the world's oldest rodeos, which has been held annually since 1888. In addition to the rodeo action, visitors enjoy arts and crafts booths, a parade, and a spectacular fireworks display.

Navajo Nation Fair In September, more than 200,000 people descend on Window Rock for the world's largest American Indian fair. Highlights include dancing competitions, livestock shows, rodeos, and jewelry displays.

Navajo Nation Fair

Sedona Jazz on the Rocks World-class jazz performers travel to Sedona in September to play an outdoor concert in the spectacular red rock country.

La Fiesta de los Chiles Don't bother coming to this October event in Tucson unless you like hot, spicy food. Almost everything you'll eat there includes hot chile peppers, from jalapeño pizza to Thai chile salad to chocolate chile ice cream. There are also displays of crafts with a chile theme and some hot music as well.

Arizona State Fair This two-week extravaganza in Phoenix features everything from exhibits of rabbits to monster truck competitions. It takes place in late October and early November.

Thunderbird Balloon Classic Watch 150 hot air balloons float through the blue Arizona sky at this November event in Scottsdale.

Festival of Lights Boat Parade Dozens of decorated boats cruise Lake Powell each December, their lights dancing on the water.

STATE STARS

Edward Abbey (1927–1989), a novelist and essayist, wrote belligerent, funny books calling for the protection of the wilderness. Abbey first earned acclaim in 1968 for *Desert Solitaire*, about the year he spent working as a park ranger. His moving descriptions of the desert and arguments for its preservation inspired the environmental movement. In later books such as *The Monkey Wrench Gang* and *The Journey Home*, Abbey continued to urge people to fight for the wilderness. Abbey lived in Oracle.

Cesar Chavez (1927–1993) was a labor leader who led the first successful strike by California farm workers. Chavez, who was born in Yuma, was employed as a farm worker in his youth. In the 1950s, he became a community organizer, putting together voter registration drives and helping people in their interactions with the government. Later, his attention turned to labor organizing, and he founded what would become the United Farm Workers. In 1965, the union went on strike against California grape growers. Chavez organized an international boycott of California grapes in support of the strikers. After several years, the grape growers finally signed contracts with the union. Never before had a farm workers' union in California obtained contracts.

Cochise (1815–1874) was a Chiracahua Apache leader. In 1861, he was falsely accused of kidnapping a white child, which started a war. For several years, Cochise led battles against U.S. troops, fighting to retain native land. He finally surrendered in 1872.

Ted Danson

Ted Danson (1947–   ) is an actor most famous for starring in the long-running television show *Cheers*. He earned two Emmy Awards for his portrayal of the baseball player turned bartender. The amiable actor has also appeared in such films as *Three Men and a Baby* and *Cousins*. Danson grew up in Flagstaff.

Geronimo (1829–1909), a Chiracahua Apache leader, was born in what is now Clifton, Arizona. After his family was killed in 1858, he began raiding Mexican and American settlements. He became known as a great warrior. During the 1880s, Geronimo led a band of renegades who refused to stay on the San Carlos Reservation. In 1886, he was finally captured and sent to a prison camp in Florida. In his later years, he toured with a Wild West show.

Barry Goldwater (1909–1998) was a blunt-spoken politician who began the modern conservative political movement in America. Goldwater, a native of Phoenix, was president of his family's department store chain before being elected to the first of his six terms in the U.S. Senate. In 1964, he was the Republican candidate for president. Although he lost in a landslide, over time more and more people began agreeing with his opposition to government spending and regulations.

Barry Goldwater

R. C. Gorman (1932–   ), who was born in Chinle on the Navajo Reservation, is a leading Native American artist, famed for his free-flowing expressiveness. Gorman was one of the first Indian artists to incorporate European styles in his depiction of Native American subjects, which has made him very influential among younger Indian artists. He was also the first Native American to own his own gallery.

Helen Hull Jacobs (1908–1997) was one of the greatest tennis players of the early twentieth century, famed for her speed and drive to win. She

ranked among the top ten players in the world every year from 1928 to 1940 and won the U.S. National Championship four years in a row. Jacobs was born in Globe.

Helen Hull Jacobs

Barbara Kingsolver (1955–   ) is an esteemed novelist who lives in Tucson. In works such as *The Bean Trees* and *Animal Dreams*, Kingsolver uses poetic language to bring her characters and their complex relationships to life. Kingsolver's novels often refer to political and environmental issues, but she has also written nonfiction books such as *High Tide in Tucson* that confront these issues more directly.

Eusebio Francisco Kino (1645–1711), a Catholic priest born in Italy, founded 29 missions in northern Mexico and southern Arizona. In his work as a missionary, Kino introduced cattle, sheep, and wheat to the region. Kino was also a mapmaker who gained fame for a map that showed that southern California was not an island, as Europeans thought at the time.

Percival Lowell (1855–1916) was an astronomer who founded the Lowell Observatory in Flagstaff, Arizona. Lowell, who came from a prominent Massachusetts family, spent his early career as a diplomat in Asia. In 1894, he set up a telescope in Flagstaff, because it offered a clear view far from the city lights. He devoted the rest of his life to observing the planets. Lowell is most famous for claiming incorrectly that Mars held intelligent life and for predicting the existence of another planet in the solar system. This ninth planet, Pluto, was discovered by astronomers at the Lowell Observatory after Lowell's death.

Charles Mingus (1922–1979) was an innovative jazz bassist and composer who changed how the double bass is played. Instead of just using it as a rhythm instrument, he played melody and percussion on it as well. In the 1940s and 1950s, Mingus played with many jazz legends, including Louis Armstrong and Charlie Parker. He later led his own group, the Charles Mingus Jazz Workshop. Some of his compositions, such as "Goodbye Pork Pie Hat" and "Wednesday Night Prayer Meeting," have become classics. Mingus was born in Nogales.

Charles Mingus

Sandra Day O'Connor (1930–   ) was the first female justice on the U.S. Supreme Court. O'Connor was born in El Paso, Texas, and spent much of her childhood on her family's ranch near Duncan, Arizona. She worked as a lawyer and assistant attorney general in Phoenix before becoming an Arizona state senator. Later, as a judge on the Maricopa County Superior Court and the Arizona Court of Appeals, she earned a reputation for fairness and hard work. In 1981, President Ronald Reagan made history when he appointed her to the Supreme Court.

John Wesley Powell (1834–1902) led the first expedition down the Colorado River all the way through the Grand Canyon. Powell, who was born in New York, lost an arm while fighting for the Union during the Civil War. Powell led expeditions through the canyon in 1869 and 1871–1872. His mesmerizing book, *Explorations of the Colorado River of the West*, made the canyon famous. Later Powell became head of the U.S. Geological Survey.

William Rehnquist (1924–   ) is the chief justice of the U.S. Supreme Court. Rehnquist, a Wisconsin native, set up his legal practice in Phoenix in 1953. He eventually began working for the U.S. Justice Department and in 1971 was appointed to the Supreme Court. Rehnquist soon proved himself one of the Court's most conservative members. In 1986, he was named chief justice.

William Rehnquist

Marty Robbins (1925–1982), one of the most successful country singers of all time, was born in Glendale. Robbins began performing in clubs around Glendale in the late 1940s, and by 1950, he had his own television show in Phoenix. Robbins had hit after hit through the 1950s and 1960s. In 1959, "El Paso" reached number one on both the country and the pop charts. Robbins eventually had 94 songs climb onto the country charts, the eighth-highest total ever.

Marty Robbins

Linda Ronstadt (1946–   ) is a popular singer whose work has ranged from country to rock to opera to Latin. Ronstadt first hit it big with her 1974 album *Heart Like a Wheel*, which sold 2 million copies and produced a string of hits, including "You're No Good" and "When Will I Be Loved," that climbed both the pop and the country charts. In 1987, Ronstadt recorded a Spanish-language album, *Canciones de Mi Padre* (*Songs of My Father*), which earned her a Grammy Award. Ronstadt, a native of Tucson, has won a total of ten Grammies.

Leslie Marmon Silko (1948–   ) is a critically acclaimed novelist and poet who explores the world of Native Americans. In her first novel, *Ceremony*, Silko weaves traditional Indian stories into her tale of a man trying to keep his sanity after returning home from the horrors of World War II. Another novel, *Almanac of the Dead*, deals with the long history of mistreatment of Native Americans. Silko lives in Tucson.

Louis Tewanima

Louis Tewanima (1879–1969) was a runner who held the American record in the 10,000-meter race for 52 years. Tewanima was born in Shongopovi on the Hopi reservation. He attended the Carlisle Indian School in Pennsylvania, where his graceful running was soon noticed. Tewanima won the silver medal in the 10,000 meters at the 1912 Olympics. In 1954, he was named to the All-Time United States Olympic Track and Field Team, and three years later he was the first person inducted into the Arizona Sports Hall of Fame.

Morris Udall (1922–1998) was a highly respected politician who represented Arizona in Congress for 30 years. Udall was known for his sense of humor and his willingness to work with members of both parties. His accomplishments include helping establish wilderness areas and working for campaign finance reform and civil rights legislation. Udall was born in St. Johns.

Morris Udall

TOUR THE STATE

Monument Valley (Kayenta) A 17-mile scenic drive takes visitors past striking red buttes and spires.

Hubbell Trading Post National Historic Site (Ganado) Since 1876, Navajo have been bringing such items as rugs and jewelry to this post to exchange for food, tools, and other supplies. Besides seeing outstanding crafts, you can often watch artists at work.

Meteor Crater (Winslow) Nearly 50,000 years ago, a meteor slammed into Earth, creating this huge hole in the ground 570 feet deep and 4,100 feet across. It is the best-preserved meteor crater on the planet.

Navajo Bridge (Lees Ferry) Brave visitors can walk across this narrow 909-foot-long bridge that looms 470 feet above the Colorado River at Marble Canyon.

Pipe Spring National Monument (Fredonia) Get a taste of frontier life at this restored fort and ranch from 1871.

Grand Canyon National Park (Tusayan) This massive chasm, the most famous natural site in the United States, features stunning views and steep trails.

Sunset Crater Volcano National Monument (Flagstaff) The Lava Flow Trail at the base of this volcanic cone that last erupted about 750 years ago takes visitors past hardened gnarly lava. Amazingly, some plants have managed to grow in this strange moonscape.

Museum of Northern Arizona (Flagstaff) Exquisite Anasazi pottery, colorful Hopi Kachina dolls, and a detailed display on the geology of the Grand Canyon are just a few of the draws at this excellent museum.

Jerome State Historic Park (Jerome) Located in a mansion built for "Rawhide Jimmy" Douglas, the local mining king, this park will tell you all about the history of Jerome, an unusual town that clings to the side of a mountain.

Chapel of the Holy Cross (Sedona) This powerful modern church is built among the red rocks of Sedona.

London Bridge (Lake Havasu City) This bridge spanned the river Thames in London for about 140 years before being taken apart and transported to the Mohave Desert.

Heard Museum (Phoenix) You can check out a Navajo hogan, listen to Native American music, and even do your own beadwork at the leading museum of southwestern Indians.

Desert Botanical Garden (Phoenix) People have been living in the Sonoran Desert for thousands of years. Find out how they used the unusual desert plants by making your own paintbrush out of a yucca frond or pounding mesquite beans into flour. You'll also find out how these plants have adapted to their severe environment.

Hall of Flame Museum of Firefighting (Phoenix) At this museum, you can climb aboard a fire engine from 1916 and get a good look at more than a hundred others. The Hall of Flame also boasts the world's largest collection of firefighting gear.

Casa Grande Ruins National Monument (Coolidge) The Hohokam built this massive four-story high structure around A.D. 1350. It is the largest prehistoric building in Arizona.

Yuma Territorial Prison (Yuma) After this prison was built in 1876, it became known as the Hellhole of Arizona. Touring it today, you'll hear stories of the men and women who suffered in its 120 degree heat and of their escape attempts.

Tonto National Monument (Roosevelt) Climb through the beautiful Superstition Mountains to see the ruins of buildings the Salado people built in a cave nearly 700 years ago.

Saguaro National Monument (Tucson) A drive through this park will take you past vast stands of towering saguaro cacti. If you come in the early morning or evening, you might catch a glimpse of some of the many animals that make their home in the desert, such as roadrunners, jackrabbits, and desert tortoises.

Tombstone Pretend you're one of the Earp boys as you walk down Tombstone's wooden sidewalks past buildings where bullet holes are still visible. The offices of the *Tombstone Epitaph*, the newspaper that chronicled all the mayhem, display the paper's original printing press and other memorabilia.

Tumacacori National Historical Park (Tubac) The ruins of this simple, weighty mission church built around 1800 evoke a time when Spanish missionaries were the only non-Indians in Arizona.

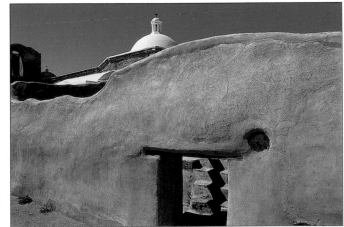

Tumacacori National Historical Park

FUN FACTS

Sometimes it's hard to know what time it is in Arizona. It is the only state in the Union that doesn't participate in daylight savings time. In April, Utah to the north and New Mexico to the east suddenly jump an hour ahead, but Arizona doesn't. The sprawling Navajo Reservation, however, does use daylight savings time. To complicate matters further, the Hopi Reservation, which is completely surrounded by the Navajo lands, sticks with the rest of Arizona and stays on standard time. So when you go from New Mexico to Arizona in the summer, you lose an hour, but when you enter Navajo country you jump ahead an hour—and then you go back an hour when you cross into Hopi land!

Arizona is the site of the nation's largest mass escape from a prisoner-of-war camp. During World War II, German prisoners were held in what is now Phoenix's Papago Park. On Christmas Eve, 1944, 25 Germans escaped after having spent months digging a 180-foot-long tunnel. Three of them had studied maps of Arizona and planned to build a raft and sail it down the Salt River to Mexico. Unfortunately for them, when they got to the river, it was bone dry. All of the escapees were eventually recaptured.

FIND OUT MORE

You can learn a lot more about Arizona at your local library. Here are some titles to get you started.

BOOKS

Aaseng, Nathan. *Navajo Code Talkers*. New York: Walker & Co., 1992.

Bonvillain, Nancy. *The Navajos*. Brookfield, CT: Millbrook, 1995.

Frasier, Mary Ann. *In Search of the Grand Canyon*. New York: Henry Holt and Company, 1995.

Hermann, Spring. *R. C. Gorman: Navajo Artist*. Springfield, NJ: Enslow, 1995.

Huber, Peter. *Sandra Day O'Connor*. New York: Chelsea House, 1990.

Rodruiguez, Consuela. *Cesar Chavez*. New York: Chelsea House, 1991.

Sears, Bryan P., and G. S. Prentzas. *The Hopi Indians*. New York: Chelsea House, 1994.

Thompson, Kathleen. *Arizona*. Austin, TX: Raintree-Steck-Vaughn, 1996.

Warren, Scott. *Cities in the Sand: The Ancient Civilizations of the Southwest*. San Francisco: Chronicle Books, 1992.

VIDEOS

Ancient Indian Cultures of Northern Arizona. Finley Holiday Film, 1998.

Arizona. Travel Preview Series, 1999.

Rainbow of Stone: A Journey through Deep Time in the Grand Canyon. Terra Productions, 1996.

INTERNET

www.state.az.us
   The official website of the state of Arizona is chock-full of information about the state. It also has many useful links to other sites.

www.azcentral.com
   Read the *Arizona Republic*, the state's largest newspaper, online to find out what's currently going on in Arizona.

INDEX

Chart, graph, and illustration page numbers are in boldface.